Johnson's

sleep

London, New York, Munich, Melbourne, Delhi

Text by Katy Holland
For my mum, Lesley-ann

Senior editor Julia North
Senior art editors Glenda Fisher, Hannah Moore
Project editor Anne Esden
Project art editor Claire Legemah
DTP designer Karen Constanti
Production controller Heather Hughes
Managing editor Anna Davidson
Managing art editor Emma Forge
Photography art direction Sally Smallwood
Photography Ruth Jenkinson

Category publisher Corinne Roberts

First published in Great Britain in 2004 by
Dorling Kindersley Limited, A Penguin Company
80 Strand, London WC2R 0RL

2 4 6 8 10 9 7 5 3 1

Every effort has been made to ensure that the information contained in this book is complete and accurate. However, neither the publisher nor the authors are engaged in rendering professional advice or services to the individual reader. The ideas, procedures and suggestions contained in this book are not intended as a substitute for consulting with your healthcare provider. All matters regarding the health of you and your baby require medical supervision. Neither the authors nor the publisher shall be liable or responsible for any loss or damage allegedly arising from any information or suggestion in this book.

A CIP catalogue record for this book is available from the British Library

ISBN 0 7513 3886 9

Reproduced by Colourscan, Singapore
Printed by Graphicom, Italy

See our complete catalogue at
www.dk.com

A message to parents from

Johnson's

The most precious gift in the world is a new baby. To your little one, you are the centre of the universe. And by following your most basic instincts to touch, hold and talk to your baby, you provide the best start to a happy, healthy life.

Our baby products encourage parents to care for and nurture their children through the importance of touch, developing a deep, loving bond that transcends all others.

Parenting is not an exact science, nor is it a one-size-fits-all formula. For more than a hundred years Johnson & Johnson has supported the healthcare needs of parents and healthcare professionals, and we understand that all parents feel more confident in their role when they have information they can trust.

That is why we offer this book as our commitment to you to provide scientifically sound, professionally reviewed guidance on the important topics of pregnancy, babycare and child development.

As you read through this book, the most important thing to remember is this: you know your baby better than anyone else. By watching, listening and having confidence in your natural ability, you will know how to use the information you have in your hands, for the benefit of the baby in your arms.

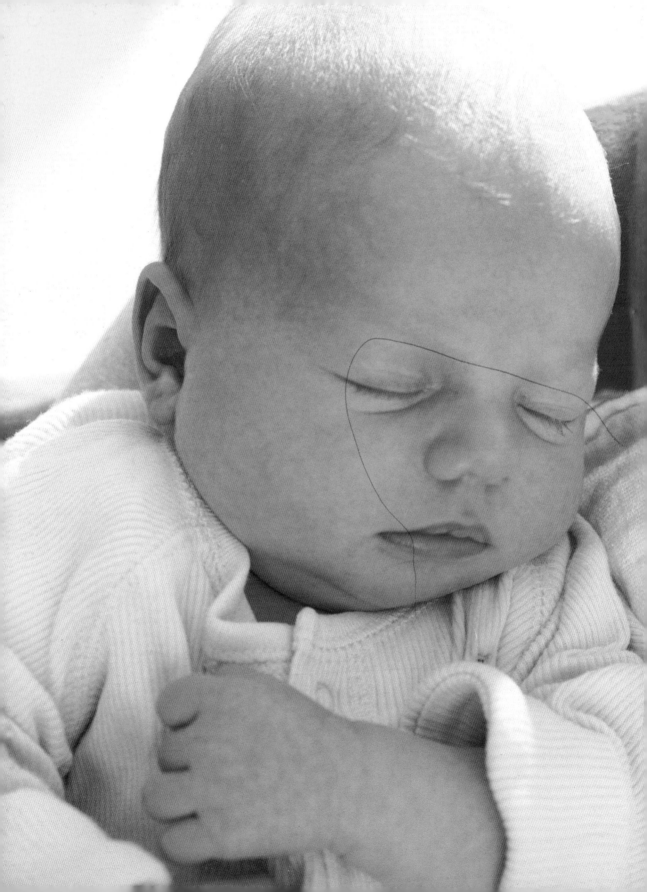

Contents

1 What happens when my baby sleeps? **6**

2 Where should my baby sleep? **12**

3 The first few weeks **22**

4 Encouraging good sleeping habits **30**

5 The benefits of routine **38**

6 Sleep and your toddler **46**

7 The pre-school years **52**

8 Special situations **56**

Useful contacts **62**

Index **63**

Acknowledgments **64**

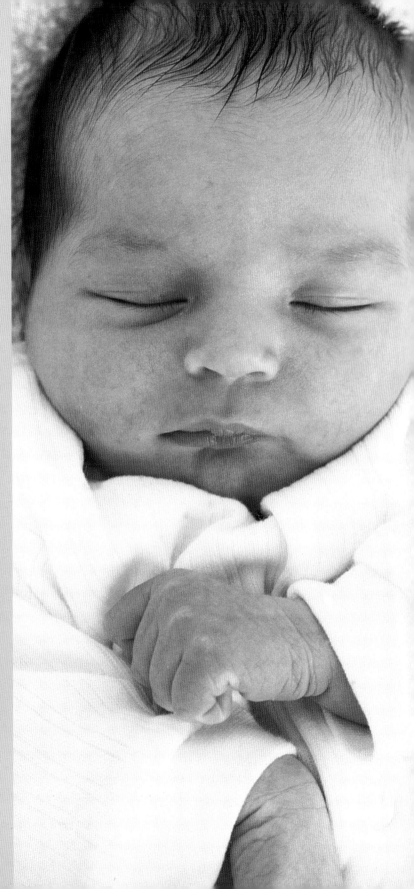

" I love to watch my baby when he's asleep. Sometimes, he lies **still and peaceful**, and other times he **wriggles and twitches**. He even smiles as though he's having a lovely dream. **"**

EVA is mum to three-week-old Jake

1

What happens when my baby sleeps?

Sleep is a precious commodity – both for your baby and for you. And it's not just the quantity of sleep that's important, it's the quality, too. Sleep affects every aspect of our lives, and understanding what happens when we sleep is the first step to helping your baby develop healthy sleeping habits that will benefit the whole family.

Sleep stages

When he is born (and even before he is born), your baby's days are divided into periods of sleep and wakefulness. His sleep periods consist of two distinct states, which are very similar to those stages that we all experience.

● **Active sleep (so-called in newborn babies), also known as rapid–eye–movement (REM) sleep** If you watch your baby while he is sleeping, you will notice that there are times when, under his eyelids, his eyes flick frantically from side to side and he may frown, or wriggle his fingers and toes. This is REM, or "dream", sleep.

Although the full function of REM sleep remains a mystery, it is known to be essential to the development and maintenance of the brain.

Studies show that it is particularly important for learning, and helps in the formation of memories.

Newborn babies spend around half their sleep time in REM sleep, whereas in adulthood REM sleep accounts only for approximately 20 per cent of our sleep. Unlike adults and older children, newborn babies fall directly into REM sleep, a pattern that continues until they are around three months old.

● **Quiet sleep (newborns) or non-REM sleep** When your baby is not in REM sleep, his sleep is more peaceful and his brain is less active. This stage is non-REM sleep, and consists of four phases

REM AND NON-REM SLEEP
Your newborn spends around half the time that he's asleep in REM sleep (left). During this stage, his eyes flick beneath his eyelids, or he may twitch his fingers and toes. The rest of the time, he's in deep, non-REM sleep (right), when he's very quiet and still.

Checklist

Sleep is absolutely vital to your baby's physical and mental development. While he sleeps:

• the cells in his brain and body are multiplying rapidly, and his growth hormones are stimulated into action

• the calories from his milk convert into energy for growth and warmth, and build muscle and body tissue

• his body is producing white blood cells, which are essential to help his immune system fight infection

• his brain is very active, expanding and making new connections at an amazing rate.

of gradually deepening sleep: drowsiness, light sleep, deep sleep and very deep sleep. Like you, your baby will go through these phases in "cycles", alternating periods of REM and non-REM sleep, throughout the night. During the progression into deepest sleep, your baby is less active and his breathing slows. Unlike during REM sleep, very little, if any, dreaming occurs in this stage.

Sleep cycles

Your newborn sleeps in cycles of around 50 or 60 minutes of REM and non-REM sleep. These cycles become longer as he matures, so that in later

childhood they will last around 90 minutes, like those of an adult. Adults and babies go through several sleep cycles every night. At the end of each one, we awaken very briefly.

These semi-awakenings may or may not become complete awakenings, depending on whether we feel secure in our surroundings or there is something disturbing us. Normally, we drop back off again.

Like you, your baby wakes up several times in the night as part of his natural sleep cycle. If he is able to lull himself back to sleep, this stirring will pass unnoticed. However, if he can't go back to sleep without help from you, he may become fully awake and cry. This is a common reason for disturbed nights, and one that can be solved by teaching your baby how to soothe himself back to sleep (see pages 30–37).

How many hours?

Parents commonly ask how much sleep their baby needs. But the answer is not straightforward, because every baby's sleep needs are different. The following is a very rough guide – and bear in mind that your baby is unlikely to be "average".

• **Newborn to two months**
Newborns have no regular pattern and may sleep from as little as 10½ hours to 20 hours out of 24.

Typical sleep stage progression

This chart shows a typical sleep cycle in older infants, showing the stages from deep non-REM sleep through to brief wakings from light sleep and dreaming. If your child is able to fall back to sleep on his own, he will not be disturbed. But if he needs your help, he's likely to cry for you.

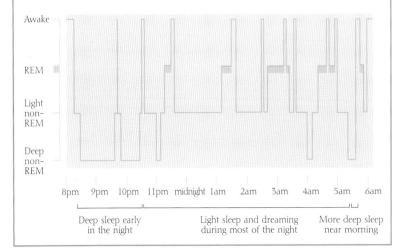

	Awake
	REM
	Light non-REM
	Deep non-REM

8pm 9pm 10pm 11pm midnight 1am 2am 3am 4am 5am 6am

Deep sleep early in the night

Light sleep and dreaming during most of the night

More deep sleep near morning

- **Two to three months** Night-time sleep averages about nine hours, with around an additional five hours of naps through the day.
- **Six months** By six months, the average baby will sleep around 10 to 11 hours at night, with around two to four hours of naps.
- **12 months onwards** Total night-time sleep will be around 11½ hours, with around 2½ hours of naps.
- **Toddlers** The need for daytime naps starts to taper off at around the age of three, although around 25 per cent of children continue to nap at the age of five years. He will probably spend around 11½ hours asleep at night, and his naps will

Sleep facts

- Sleep is essential in children of all ages for different types of health and development: physical, emotional and cognitive. It has an impact on your baby's mood, learning and behaviour. Conversely, health-related factors and developmental issues have an important impact on sleep and sleep patterns in children.

- Sleep is both an innate, biologically based phenomenon and a learned behaviour that is influenced by environment, social and cultural considerations, and life events. Because much of sleep behaviour is learned, it follows that you are your baby's best teacher when it comes to establishing good sleep skills.

- Sleep patterns and behaviours in babies and children are not static, but change and evolve across childhood in a predictable way.

- Although sleep patterns and needs are largely consistent across babies and children at the same stage of development, there is still considerable variation from one child to the next.

- Sleep is a family concern. Not only do parents and families have an impact upon the development of healthy sleep in their children, but sleep problems in children affect the whole family. Therefore, the development of healthy sleep habits may be looked upon as a partnership between you and your baby.

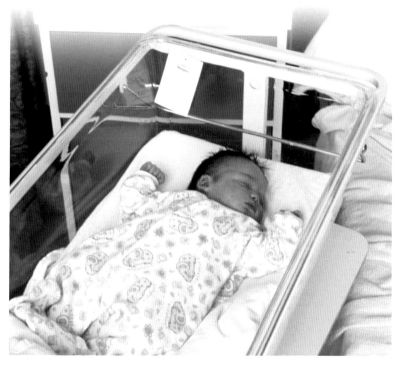

reduce from around 2½ hours (at the age of one) to 1½ hours or less (at age three).

Evolving patterns

Your baby's sleep patterns change according to his needs. A newborn will sleep in stretches of two or three hours at a time, after which he will wake up, feed and fall back to sleep again. His periods of sleep are spread throughout the day and night.

At around eight to 12 weeks, your baby's biological clock starts to develop. From here onwards, you may notice his sleep becoming more regular, and you will be able

Questions & Answers

Do premature babies have different sleep patterns?

Yes. Premature babies tend to wake more often at night than full-term infants for the first few months, and possibly up to a year. Night-waking and lighter sleep are part of a premature baby's in-built survival mechanism in that he's able to wake easily so that he can be fed. He will sleep much more than a full-term baby, and a larger proportion of his sleep time (up to 90 per cent) will be spent in REM sleep. His sleep patterns will settle in time, but they will take longer than those of a baby born at term.

Does my baby dream?

It is not known for sure whether babies dream, but it seems very likely. Dreams take place during REM sleep, and babies spend a large part of their sleep time in this sleep stage. Experts are not entirely sure why we dream; some believe that it helps the brain to process information and exercise the synapses, or pathways, between brain cells. Interestingly, our brain waves during dream sleep, as recorded by machines, are almost identical in nature to the brain waves during the hours we spend awake. This is not the case during the other phases of sleep.

to start guiding him into a day-night sleep routine. He may naturally begin to show a preference for night-time sleeping at this stage, and he'll probably spend longer periods awake and active during the day.

However, no two babies are alike. At eight weeks, some babies are sleeping for five hours at a time, while others are still waking up for feeds every two to three hours.

By around four or five months, most babies will have adopted regular patterns of waking and sleeping, which repeat every 24 hours. Your baby will benefit from having a routine, and you will be able to try

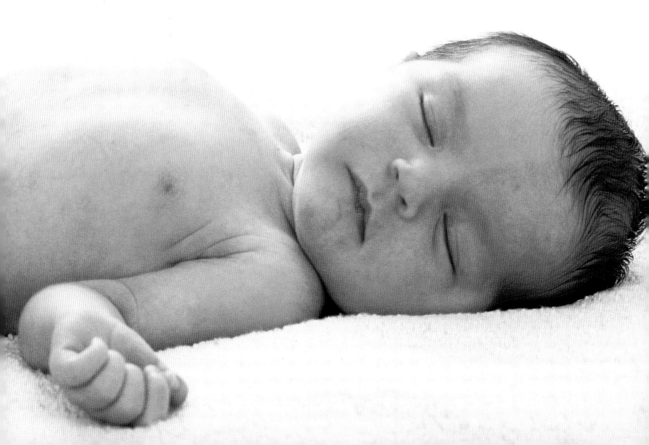

out some recommended methods for sleep training (see page 32), as he is now ready to start sleeping through the night. His sleep may naturally improve at this age because it will be regulated by his body clock, and by six months he should be able to sleep six to eight hours at night without needing a feed.

Normally, at around 10 months, a baby's sleep periods become very regular, so that he wakes up and goes to sleep at around the same time every day, and his sleep spans are longer. He will still need to take naps to "top up" his sleep, but after the age of two years, most babies will need just one nap during the day.

Healthy habits

Although your baby doesn't need to be taught how to sleep, healthy sleep habits are something he will have to learn. Whether he sleeps soundly or not depends to a great extent on what you teach him. This is not as daunting as it may sound, and the sooner you start, the easier it will be.

● **Establish a routine** Babies, toddlers and children are comforted by familiarity (see page 32). Regular bedtime habits – bathing, followed by feeding, cuddling and a little quiet time in the cot, for example - will help your baby understand that soon it will be time to go to sleep.

● **Teach your baby to fall asleep by himself** This is one of the most valuable lessons you can teach your baby. Many experts believe that, after the newborn phase, putting your baby to bed by rocking him or feeding him prevents him from developing self-soothing behaviours. Instead, they recommend putting your baby to bed when he's still awake, well-fed, sleepy and able to fall asleep without help from you.

● **Make sure he gets daytime rest** Although it is a good idea to limit the length of daytime naps to maintain a contrast between night and day, keeping your baby awake when he wants to sleep makes him overtired. He will then be harder to settle, and he will sleep more fitfully.

A RELAXING BATH
Many babies find a warm bath relaxing, which makes it a perfect way to end the day as part of a bedtime routine.

● **Be aware of your baby's needs** Respond quickly to a sudden change in your baby's sleep pattern. If he is teething or has a cold, you may need to alter his bedtime and naptime routines for a while. A baby who is ill needs plenty of cuddles and extra care. Once he's well again, return to your established routine.

● **Be consistent** Changing your baby's daytime routines and allowing him to sleep in different places, rather than just in his cot, is fine once in a while, but if it happens too often it can become a habit and lead to problems.

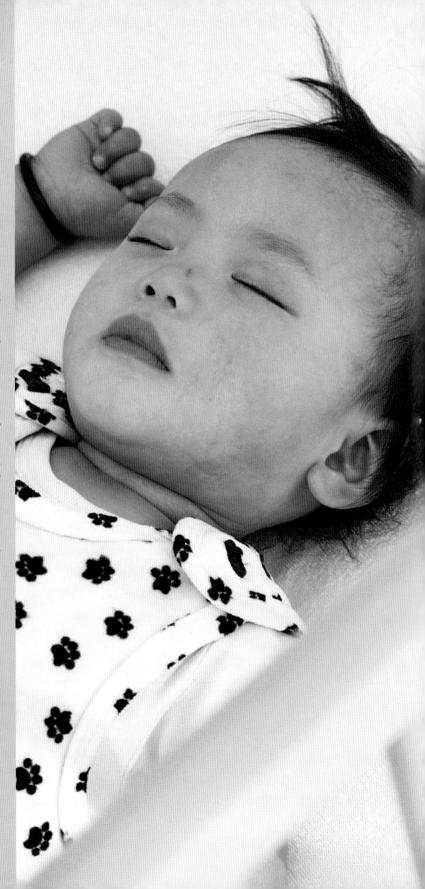

" I remember putting my baby to bed on her first night home. She looked **so tiny**, lying there in her Moses basket by my bed. Now, she sleeps quite happily **in her cot** in the nursery. "

JULIE is mum to six-month-old Alice

Where should my baby sleep?

While some parents find it hard to decide where they want their baby to sleep, others have strong opinions from the start. As long as your baby is safe and comfortable, there are no hard-and-fast rules about the best place to put your baby at night. The right arrangement for you should be wherever all your family members sleep best.

If you are undecided where your baby should sleep, weigh up the pros and cons and experiment a little. Of course, your partner – and your baby – will have their own opinions, and these will need to be taken into account.

Do remember, too, that you may find yourself changing your sleeping arrangements as your baby – and your family – grows.

A separate room?

New babies are better off sleeping near their parents during the early weeks. You might prefer to start by having your baby in a Moses basket beside your bed, and move her into her own room when she is more settled, perhaps when she's ready to move into a cot (see page 14).

Moses baskets

Moses baskets are cosy and practical, and many newborn babies seem to prefer their smaller space to the seemingly vast expanse of a cot. The carry handles allow you to transfer your Moses basket from room to room if you need to, so that you can keep a close eye on your baby. And, as you can keep the basket right by your bed, you will find it easier to comfort her and feed her at night.

Not all babies will be happy to sleep in a Moses basket, however. Just as some seem to love the confined space, others seem to hate it. If your baby is not comfortable with the fact that her arms can touch the sides, this may disturb her.

A good Moses basket should be firm but snug for your baby. They usually come with a valance that

Expert tips

If your baby shares your room:

• night feeds will be easier, because you won't have far to get out of bed to go to your baby, and you should be able to go straight back to sleep

• you should sleep more peacefully in between feeds because you won't have to worry about her, especially in the early days: Is she still breathing? Is she too hot or cold? Will I hear her?

If you put your baby to sleep in her own room from the outset:

• you will be helping her get into the habit of sleeping on her own

• you and your partner are less likely to be disturbed when your baby stirs – unless she really starts to cry or you are worried about her

• it will give you space to spend time on your own or with your partner.

Expert tips

Cot safety

● Make sure your baby's cot is safety approved. Modern cot designs are required by law to meet certain standards.

● Cot bars should be no more than 6cm (2³/₈in) apart, to avoid your baby's head and limbs getting stuck.

● Most cots have an adjustable mattress level, starting at its highest for easy access in the first months and finishing on the lowest level once your baby is able to sit up. There must be at least 50cm (20in) between the top of the mattress and the top of the cot in the lowest position and 20cm (8in) in the highest position.

● There should be no horizontal bars, which may allow your baby to climb up and possibly fall out.

● Every time you put your baby in her cot, check that the drop-side mechanism is locked. Never leave your baby in her cot with the side down.

The mattress

● The cot mattress should fit tightly – if you can slide two fingers between the cot sides or ends and the mattress, the mattress is too small.

● Mattresses are made of foam or natural fibres. Either is fine, as long as the mattress is firm, and fits snugly.

● Keep your baby's mattress well-aired and clean. Mattresses with a PVC surface or a removable washable cover are easiest to keep clean.

makes a frill around the outside, a liner and a mattress. Check that the mattress is a close fit (see left).

It's also possible to buy a stand (usually sold separately), so that you can raise the basket off the floor, keeping your baby out of harm's way and away from draughts. The stand should be sturdy and the basket must fit securely onto it.

Moses baskets are designed for babies up to 6kg or 7kg (13lb or 15lb), but once your baby begins to roll, or simply becomes too long for the basket, it's time to move her to a cot.

Cradles

You may choose to use a cradle in the early months instead of a Moses basket. Cradles have many of the advantages of Moses baskets, but

A MOSES BASKET
A Moses basket is the ideal size for your new baby, and can be carried from room to room, if necessary – although never when your baby is inside it!

they are not portable. The main difference is that they can be rocked, and your newborn may find this very soothing. If you choose a rocking cradle, make sure you can lock it into a stationary position while your baby is sleeping, and that it cannot be tipped over.

Choosing a cot

Your baby can sleep in a cot from the start, but you may prefer to wait until she is past the newborn stage before you transfer her from her Moses basket or cradle.

You can expect your baby to sleep in a cot until she's at least 18 months old, and maybe up to three years. You will know when she has outgrown it because she'll start trying to climb out of it!

There are several points to consider when choosing a cot.

● **Sturdiness** Once your baby is able to sit up and move around, a sturdy cot is a must.

● **Drop sides** One or both of the cot sides should drop for easy access. The catch mechanism needs to be very sturdy, because you will soon have a baby who can jump up and down and rattle the bars. Look for a drop mechanism that you can open with one hand if possible – you will invariably have your baby in

DROP SIDES
The drop-side mechanism on your baby's cot should be easy to operate, preferably with one hand, yet secure. Never leave the side down when your baby is in the cot.

your arms when you come to use it.

● **Teething rails** Once she can stand, your baby may want to try out her new teeth on the top of her cot. Most cots have rigid plastic strips along the top rails to protect

her from splinters and the cot from being damaged.

● **Castors** Some cots are sold with castors, which make them easier to move around for cleaning. Ensure that the castors can be locked.

A ROCKING CRADLE
The rocking movement of this type of cradle may help lull your baby to sleep. Make sure you lock it in a stationary position while she sleeps.

Multi-purpose designs

Instead of a conventional cot, you may decide to choose a cot that is designed to meet specific needs.

● **A bedside cot** has a removable side so that it can become an extension of your bed at night. This is becoming an increasingly popular way of co-sleeping (see pages 16–17).

● **A rocking cradle** can be rocked, which many babies will find soothing, or it can be locked into static mode.

● **A cot-bed** can be used as a large cot in the early years and then, by removing the sides, can be transformed into a small bed when your child is old enough. It is a good idea, but a cot-bed is usually more expensive than a normal cot, and you will at some stage need to buy a full-size bed for your child. Also, as your family grows, you might need the cot again for another baby while your older child is still using it as a bed.

Expert tips

Sharing your bed with your baby is safe as long as you follow the recommended safety guidelines.

● Do not share your bed if it is cramped, as your baby could get squashed or fall out.

● Your mattress must be firm and flat. Place your baby between you and a wall so that there is no risk of her falling out.

● Make sure that there is no space between the mattress and the wall, because your baby could become trapped.

● Never use duvets, eiderdowns, heavy blankets or bedspreads on your bed and remove your pillows.

● Do not sleep with your baby if you or your partner smokes, or if either of you have recently drunk alcohol, or are taking medication or use recreational drugs.

Sharing your bed

Sharing your bed with your baby can be a wonderful experience, but it does not suit all families. Many parents are concerned about co-sleeping because of safety issues.

You do need to be meticulous about following certain guidelines if you co-sleep (see above), so that you are not putting your baby at risk of over-heating or suffocating. One way around this is to consider a bedside cot (effectively a cot with one detachable side – see page 15), so that your baby's bed becomes an extension of yours.

Co-sleeping is a personal choice that is highly influenced by culture and lifestyle. Think about why you want to co-sleep. It's not a good idea to let your baby sleep with you just to resolve a sleep "problem". If you would prefer your baby to sleep separately from you, be consistent and stick to your decision, or you may find your baby develops habits that are difficult to reverse.

Even if you decide to have your baby in bed with you at night, it's always worth having an alternative sleeping space for her. A cot or Moses basket, for example, will come in useful for daytime naps, because when you are not with her you need somewhere secure to put her down without her being able to roll out.

The pros and cons

For those families who choose to share their bed with their baby, the arrangement can work very well. Having your baby in bed can increase the bond between you, and many parents find the experience very fulfilling.

● For some parents, co-sleeping reduces any anxieties they may have about their baby's wellbeing during the night.

● Night feeds can be far less disruptive for both you and your baby (perhaps one of the most common reasons why parents adopt this sleeping arrangement).

● Also, many parents report that they sleep better – and that their babies sleep better, too.

But there are some disadvantages.

● You may find you are disturbed more rather than less, and are awoken every time your baby grunts or wriggles.

● You may not sleep properly because you are worried about the possibility of either you or your partner rolling on top of your baby (although this is extremely unlikely unless you have been drinking alcohol or taking drugs).

● The major possible drawback of co-sleeping is that if your baby gets used to sleeping this way, you may not be able to get her used to sleeping on her own when the time comes.

● Regularly having your baby or child in bed with you can affect your intimacy with your partner in the long term.

Keeping your sleeping baby safe

To ensure that your baby sleeps in a safe environment:

● always put your baby to sleep on her back with her feet at the foot of the Moses basket or cot (see pages 20–21)

● put your baby to sleep well away from any windows, window blinds, cords or curtains

● keep household pets away

● wash your baby's bedding often

● make sure she sleeps well away from heaters and out of direct sunlight

● keep all electrical items away from your baby's sleeping space

● dress her in flame-resistant, close-fitting sleepwear.

Medical advice

Consult your doctor if:

- your baby or child has difficulty breathing or snores frequently

- your baby is sick or feverish

- your baby or child has persistent difficulties going to sleep or has trouble staying asleep

- your baby or child suddenly starts having unusual night wakings

- your baby or child wakes herself up coughing throughout the night

- an allergy, such as eczema, is affecting her sleep.

Your baby's breathing

It's only natural to worry about your baby's breathing while she sleeps. Many parents find themselves paying frequent visits to their sleeping babies to check them. This can do no harm, although it's important not to become over-anxious.

Your baby's breathing will often be irregular, and her breathing patterns will vary considerably while she sleeps. When she is in dream (REM) sleep (see page 7), she will breathe quite quickly, grunting and twitching a lot. The rest of her sleep will be much quieter, and she may be so still that it is difficult to tell whether she is breathing without you touching her.

As your baby grows, and you get to know her habits, you will be less anxious about her breathing, and you will worry less when she sleeps for longer periods without waking up.

Breathing monitors

Breathing monitors are sensitive devices that work using electronic pads under your baby's mattress. These register your baby's breathing, and an alarm goes off if there is a significant pause. Whether such

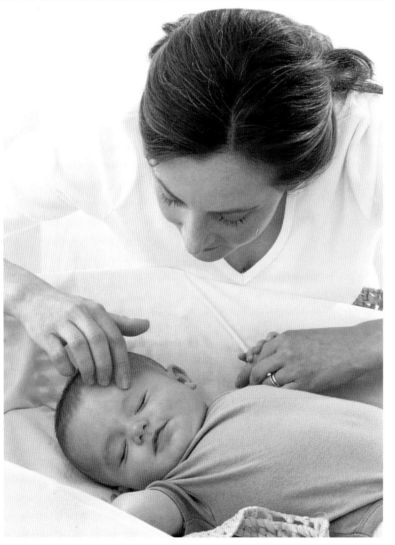

SLEEPING PEACEFULLY
Regular visits to check your baby's breathing do no harm, but try to avoid becoming over-anxious.

instruments offer reassurance is debatable. While some parents find that they do help to reduce anxiety, for others they only serve to increase their worries because of the many inevitable false alarms.

Bear in mind that breathing monitors do not prevent Sudden Infant Death Syndrome (SIDS – see pages 20–21). The Foundation for the Study of Infant Deaths (FSID – see page 62) says that it is far better to know and practise preventative methods for dealing with SIDS than to rely solely on electronic monitors.

Fortunately, SIDS is now relatively uncommon, but this is because parents follow the recommended safety advice rather than because of the use of breathing monitors.

Questions & Answers

My five-week-old baby loves sleeping in his car seat. Is it safe to let him do this?

Like many newborns, your baby may be happier in his car seat because he can adopt a more curled-up position. But the safest sleeping position for your baby is on his back, on a firm mattress, and this is very important. Although it is safe for him to sleep in his car seat under your watchful eye, you should never put him down for the night in it. Car seats are not designed as permanent sleeping places.

It's OK if your baby falls asleep in his car seat during the day if he is within your sight. Make sure that he doesn't slump over with his head down, as this can restrict his breathing and be very dangerous. Support his head by using the padded car seat head rest. When your baby is in his car seat, never put it on a high surface, as it could fall off – car seats falling from high surfaces are one of the leading causes of domestic accidents in babies.

Where should my baby sleep for her daytime naps?

It's fine to use your baby's night-time sleeping place for naps during the day. But to help her differentiate between day and night sleep, when you put her down for her nap, do not darken the room or tip-toe around the house. Exposure to daylight and daytime noises will help her to register the differences between napping and night sleep, and will help to regulate her body clock.

From cot to bed

You'll know when it's time to move your child from her cot to a "big bed". If she seems cramped or she is making attempts to climb out, she's probably ready! There is no set age or reason for doing this, although as a general guideline, she should be in a bed by the time she is around 1m (3ft) tall. Often the move comes about for a specific reason. Perhaps you need to free the cot for a new baby, in which case, try to move your toddler into her new bed several weeks before

the baby's ready for the cot to prevent your toddler feeling displaced by her sibling. It could also be that you are toilet training your toddler and she needs easy access to the bathroom.

Some children will adjust easily to this change to a big bed, while others will not (see pages 50–51). To protect your child, invest in a guard rail. This fits on to the side of the bed to prevent her from falling out as she gets used to her new sleeping arrangement.

How can I keep my baby safe?

All parents worry about the possibility of Sudden Infant Death Syndrome (SIDS), but it's important to remember that the chances of it happening to your baby are very slim. The causes of this tragic syndrome are not yet fully understood, but there are some important precautions you can take to reduce the risk significantly.

The following recommendations apply throughout your baby's first year, although they are particularly important during the first six months, when incidences of SIDS are at their highest. If your baby sleeps with a babysitter or any other carer, make sure they also follow these guidelines.

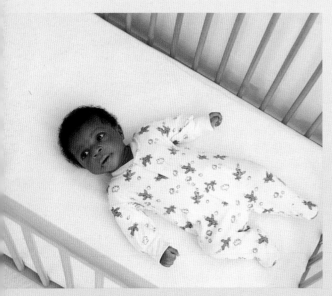

FEET TO FOOT
Always place your baby with her feet to the foot of the cot, cradle or Moses basket. This safety measure ensures that she cannot slip under or become entangled with her bedclothes, if you are using them, and allows her to wriggle free of her covers if she becomes too hot.

★ **Always put your baby down to sleep on her back** Studies have proved that putting your baby to sleep on her back significantly lowers the risk of SIDS. Once your baby is older, she will be able to turn herself onto her stomach. However, you should continue to put her to sleep on her back even if she does change position in the night.

★ **Never smoke around your baby** You should also keep her away from smoky atmospheres. Babies who are exposed to cigarette smoke are at a higher risk of dying from SIDS.

★ **Keep your baby's bedroom at the right temperature** A room temperature of around 18°C (65°F) is ideal. Over-heating can be life-threatening because your baby cannot yet regulate her own temperature properly. The best way to test if she is becoming too hot is to feel her bare tummy or the nape of her neck.

★ **Place her with her feet at the foot of the cot, Moses basket or cradle** This is vital, because it prevents your baby slipping under the covers and suffocating. You should always keep her head uncovered.

★ **Never use duvets, quilts or thick blankets**
Soft bedding can cause your baby to become over-
heated. It is best to use a sheet or one or two
layers of thin blankets that are securely tucked into
the sides and foot of the mattress, no higher than
your baby's chest. In warmer weather, take off a
layer or remove bedcovers altogether.

★ **Never use cot bumpers or a pillow** These
can contribute to over-heating, and can also
suffocate your baby. For similar reasons, you should
never leave soft toys in her cot or put your baby
to sleep on top of a cushion, bean bag or water-bed.
Also, avoid falling asleep with your baby on a sofa.

★ **Never use hot-water bottles** You should also
never use electric blankets in your baby's bed.

★ **Use a firm mattress, and clean and air
it regularly** Also make sure that there is no
gap between the edges and the sides of the cot
(see page 14).

★ **Seek medical advice promptly** if your
baby is unwell.

YOUR BABY'S BEDDING
*If you use bedding, use a sheet or one or two thin
blankets that reach no higher than your baby's
chest, securely tucked in on all sides.*

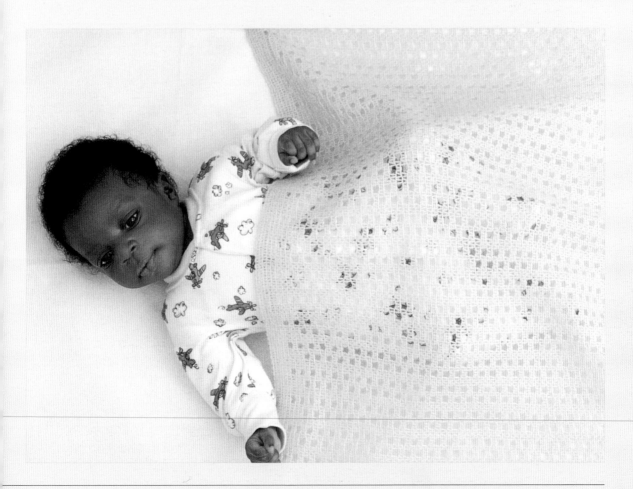

" Having our new baby home with us is **fantastic**, despite feeling tired. At the moment, she sleeps for just **two or three hours** at a time, but I know this stage won't last for too long. "

LAUREN is mum to six-week-old Minnie

3

The first few weeks

The first few weeks of your baby's life are all about adjustment – both for you and your baby. It's too soon to expect structured sleep patterns, or to try to impose a routine on him, so it makes sense to go with the flow and take your cues from your baby at this tender age, and enjoy every minute of these precious newborn days.

His first sleep

You've waited nine long months to meet your baby, and now he's here all he seems to do is sleep. But he's just doing what comes naturally. Wakefulness for the first few hours after birth, followed by a long stretch, often up to 24 hours, of very sound sleep, is the normal newborn pattern.

The majority of your baby's time at this stage will be spent sleeping and feeding, but there won't be a regular pattern to this yet. He will probably be alert only for short periods every day; he's not mature enough to benefit from longer periods of alertness, and sleep (particularly REM sleep) helps him to mature.

Gradually, these periods of wakefulness will grow longer, so that by the end of the first month he may be awake for a total of around two or three hours every day, most of it in one long stretch. He may also begin to sleep for longer periods, so that instead of one or two hours, he may be able to sleep for three or four – but this is by no means the rule.

Sleeping and feeding

Your baby uses quite a bit of energy feeding and, as milk has a soporific effect, it's very likely that he will drift back into a contented sleep as soon as he's had his fill.

It's natural for a newborn to fall asleep while sucking at the breast or on a bottle. This is fine for a while, but after the first few weeks you may want to start to change this habit so that you put him down while he's still awake but drowsy (see page 32).

An experienced feeder will take most of his feed during the first five minutes or so, and once full may doze off at the breast or bottle in contentment. But if he hasn't emptied

(see page 32).

Questions & Answers

How much sleep does my new baby need?

Your newborn gets as much sleep as his body needs, no more, no less. At this early stage of life, nothing will keep him awake if he needs to sleep, and nothing will make him sleep if he doesn't need to (although there are things you can do to help him when he's tired). Many new parents become concerned about how much or how little their newborns sleep, but you need to remember that your baby is unique and is unlikely to fit in to the "average" pattern. The simple fact is that some babies appear to need more or less sleep than others. As long as he is healthy in every way, don't worry if your newborn appears to sleep too much or too little.

"Nathan feeds greedily to begin with, followed by little bursts of comfort sucks, before falling happily asleep."

MARTHA is mum to five-week-old Nathan

Your baby's movements

While sleeping, your baby may:

● be very busy twitching, jerking, sucking, snuffling or smiling. This is normal. Even with all this activity, he is actually getting a sound sleep. These movements happen when your baby is in REM, or "dream", sleep (see page 7)

● suddenly "jump" in his sleep occasionally. This is due to a normal reflex called the "startle" or Moro reflex. It sometimes occurs for no apparent reason, although often it is a response to a loud noise or sudden jolt. It may seem worrying to you, but the reflex is actually a reassuring sign that your baby's neurological system is functioning well. It will disappear by around four months.

your breast or the bottle, gently wake him up after a few minutes and offer him some more. If he's still hungry, he'll finish his feed.

Wakey wakey!

Paediatricians recommend that newborn babies should not sleep longer than three or four hours without feeding. Although a three-month-old who sleeps through a feed would not be considered a worry, at two weeks old your baby needs a constant supply of nourishment and needs waking.

● If he doesn't wake up when you pick him up, try sitting him on your lap and gently bending him forwards.

● When he stirs, put him in a position ready to feed, with your nipple or the teat close to his lips.

● Try changing his nappy, tickling his feet, or brushing his cheek with your nipple or the teat.

● If all attempts fail, leave him a bit longer and then try again. But never let him go more than five hours without a feed. Occasionally, chronic sleepiness can interfere with your baby's feeds so much that it threatens his wellbeing. If you are worried, see your doctor.

Sleeping and crying

Your baby cries because it is the only way he can communicate – it's his way of telling you he's hungry, in pain, in need of a cuddle, or simply sleepy. At first, it's hard to interpret your baby's different cries, but as you get to know him, you'll respond to them more easily.

Some experts believe crying before going to sleep may be a way of working off energy before settling down. Whatever the cause, it is very common behaviour, and the best way to deal with it is to comfort your baby, and help him to relax and learn to soothe himself to sleep (see pages 26–27).

Using a dummy

If your baby cries a lot and sucks passionately every time you offer him your (clean) finger, even when you know that he is not hungry, a dummy may be a help. But in order that it does not become a habit, you should aim to use it only during the early months, and try to restrict it to bedtimes only.

The advantages

- A dummy can soothe your baby to sleep, and comfort him.
- If he keeps hold of the dummy, he may be less likely to wake up after a disturbance or during the lighter stages of his sleep cycle.

The disadvantages

- Your baby may begin to rely on a dummy, so it will be hard to limit its use.
- Dummies often fall out during sleep, disturbing your baby. He will probably start crying until you come and find it again.
- Dummies can limit sound-making, and may stop him exploring toys with his mouth later (an important part of his development).

Questions & Answers

Should I leave my newborn baby to cry?

Leaving your baby to "cry it out" is not advisable, particularly for the first few weeks of life. At this early stage, your baby needs you to respond to his needs promptly. You cannot "spoil" him by giving him attention; in fact, the more attention he gets, you are letting him know that he is valued and that his needs are important. In a few months, when you have got to know your baby, you may decide to leave him to cry for certain short periods at a time – for example, if you are "sleep training" and you know that he isn't crying out of pain, hunger or discomfort. But during the first few weeks, your baby will not benefit from this technique.

Inconsolable and excessive crying

A baby who cries regularly and inconsolably for long periods, usually at the end of the day, is often described as having "colic", which experts now believe may be simply an extreme form of normal crying. Your baby could be overtired or over-stimulated, and once he's started crying, he doesn't know how to stop.

It can be upsetting to see your baby in distress and not be able to soothe him,

A SOOTHING HOLD
Lay your baby across your forearm and, keeping a steadying grasp between his legs, gently rub or pat his back.

but colic is not serious, and it does no long-term damage. By three or four months, it will have stopped. A colicky baby may cry himself to sleep, but stay with him, preferably in a darkened, quiet room. Also:

- try a "colic dance", rocking him up and down while swaying your hips
- gently rub his abdomen, or pat his back while holding him across your forearm or up against your shoulder
- give him a bath, but stop if he becomes more agitated
- give him a relaxing massage.

How can I help my newborn sleep?

Sometimes, your new baby will fall asleep at the drop of a hat, but there will be other occasions when he refuses to settle, waking up and crying every time you put him down. Bear in mind that he hasn't long left the warm, cosy and secure environment of your womb; it can take some time to adapt to his strange new world. The key to coping in the early days is to help him feel comfortable and secure, creating a soothing environment for him.

USE A SLING
The more you can hold your new baby close, the more secure and settled he'll be. A sling helps you carry him, while keeping both hands free.

Ways to soothe your newborn

★ **Calming movement** When he was in the womb, your baby was lulled by the motion of you going about your daily business. Out of the womb, movement still has this effect on him. Rocking, swaying and patting while cuddled up in your arms will all contribute to contentment – and sleep – during these early weeks. After a few months, it is best to help your baby to learn to self-soothe and fall asleep on his own. But for now, he needs you.

★ **Gentle sound** In the womb, your baby was used to hearing the comforting sounds of your heartbeat, the gurgling of your stomach, and the soft tones of your voice. Now he's born, sleeping may be difficult without some background noise. He might like you talking quietly, singing or humming to him. Or he may be soothed by the rhythmic hum of a fan or the washing machine or strains of music from a radio. You could even play him a recording of womb sounds.

★ **Helping him feel secure** Because your baby is used to being curled up in a tight space, the vast expanse of a cot may make him feel insecure. If your baby seems uncomfortable in a cot, then a cradle, a Moses basket or a pram can be used to provide a snug fit that's closer to the nine-month-long embrace in the womb. For added security, try swaddling (see page 28).

★ **A full tummy** If possible, try to make the last feed you give your baby before bedtime a full one. If he nods off before he has had enough, change his position, tickle his toes and rouse him so that he can finish the feed. Otherwise, you may find he will soon wake up again for his second course.

★ **Soothing smells** Your baby has a very keen sense of smell and, in particular, he will find your individual scent very comforting. So, you could try stuffing a muslin square or a handkerchief into your shirt for a short while so that it smells of you and then placing it safely in his cot, Moses basket or cradle.

SING TO HIM
He loves the sound of your voice, and he's trying hard to focus on your face. Try singing to him, and gently swaying your hips from side to side as you cradle him in your arms.

GO FOR A WALK
The fresh air and the sights and sounds of the great outdoors will soon tire your baby. He'll also be soothed by the steady movement of the pushchair.

A GOOD FEED
Your baby will settle well if he's feeling full. If he empties one breast and still seems hungry, offer him the other side. Try winding him before putting him down.

Swaddling your newborn

Some newborns are startled by the jerky movements of their arms and legs and sleep much better if they are wrapped up snugly in a thin blanket or sheet. Some babies might not like this, but for others it works wonders. Swaddling is only suitable for newborn babies. Once your baby starts to move about, it is not a safe way for him to sleep because he can loosen the blanket or sheet and become tangled. Don't swaddle your baby if the room is much warmer than the ideal temperature of 18°C (65°F) because he may become over-heated – one of the risk factors of SIDS (see pages 20–21).

SECURELY WRAPPED
Swaddling can help your newborn baby feel secure and settled.

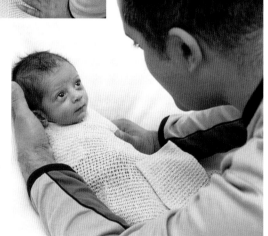

- Fold the thin blanket or sheet in half. Lay your baby down upon it, with the back of his neck level with the folded edge.

- Bring one side of the blanket or sheet up and over your baby's body, pulling it taught, then tucking it securely under him.

- Repeat with the other side, then fold the point beyond his feet loosely under his bottom. Once your baby is swaddled and calm, you can put him down. **Always put him to sleep on his back and never cover his head**.

From six weeks

During the first weeks with your baby, there will be no pattern to his sleeping and waking, and you will not be able to start any sort of routine. Your best strategy at this stage is simply to "go with the flow".

From six weeks of age, however, you may notice that he starts to become more settled, and there are ways that you can begin to help him become a good sleeper. Good sleeping habits that can be established early on will benefit both you and your baby later on.

- **Spot your baby's sleep cues** Many babies become fussy or cry when they are tired, while others rub their eyes, pull their ears or stare into space. Your baby may also turn his face away from objects or people, or bury his face into your chest. This is the time to put him down for bed or a nap, when he first lets you know he's tired.

- **Teach him the difference between night and day** You can do this by encouraging him to be more active during the day, and by putting him down for daytime naps in a room that is not too dark, and where he can hear normal daily sounds. By contrast, keep his night wakings calm and quiet, with dimmed lights and a minimum of talking or stimulation.

- **Help him learn how to self-soothe** Your newborn may like to be rocked, fed or cuddled to sleep, and to begin with you should go with whatever calms and soothes him. But, eventually, your baby needs to learn to settle by himself. By around three months he will come to recognize and depend upon any comforting techniques you may have been using as part of his settling routine and may be reluctant to give them up. So, aim to stop using these techniques before they become a habit in order to allow him to learn to go to sleep on his own (see page 32).

● **Try to be realistic about your baby's sleep patterns** Remember that your baby will not be able to sleep for long stretches at a time for the first few months, and accept that, to begin with at least, your nights will be disturbed.

DAYTIME NAP
The Moses basket is best for a daytime nap, but don't darken the room or worry about being quiet around her.

Looking after yourself

Lack of sleep affects every aspect of your life, so it's vital that you look after yourself, because if you suffer, so does your family. You need to:

● ask for help from your partner or someone close to you, so that you can have a break from your baby to catch up on some sleep, or just to relax in the bath

● accept all offers of help with domestic chores, school runs or babysitting

● ignore the housework when you are tired and try to rest or sleep while your baby sleeps, if you can

● try waking your baby up to feed him when you are ready to go to sleep for the night. If you wait for him to wake, you'll be losing sleeping time, and if you go to sleep for an hour and then he wakes, you have disturbed your sleeping patterns unnecessarily

● feed your newborn as soon as he wakes up and begins to cry

● leave some made-up bottles in the fridge, if you are bottle-feeding, together with a vacuum flask full of hot water, to minimize your workload in the night

● share the night-shift with your partner – if you are breastfeeding, you could try expressing milk once your baby is six weeks old so he can help with feeds, too.

" We've hung a brightly coloured **musical mobile** over Susannah's cot. I always turn it on as I say goodnight, and she usually falls asleep listening to its gentle **lullaby.**"

JAN is mum to four-month-old Susannah

4

Encouraging good sleeping habits

From around two months old, you may recognize a change in your baby's sleeping patterns. She will probably have more periods during the day when she's showing an interest in her surroundings. At night, she may be sleeping for longer stretches. This is the ideal time to start to encourage her to adopt good sleeping habits.

Changing patterns

By two months, your baby will be alert for longer periods during the day, and she may also be starting to sleep for longer stretches at night. A rhythm to her sleeping and waking times will soon emerge and, over the coming weeks, you will probably see these patterns taking a definite shape.

At six months old, most babies' sleep is consolidated into one longer sleep at night and several shorter sleeps during the day. There are a number of factors that contribute to these changes in your baby's sleeping patterns.

● Her sleep-wake cycles are becoming less dependent on hunger: as her stomach capacity grows, she can go longer without needing to feed. She may even drop one of her night feeds altogether. By six months, when solid foods account for a substantial part of her diet, most – but not all – babies will sleep for a six-hour stretch without waking.

● Your baby's internal body clock is beginning to tick. This means that she will spend more time awake during the day and more time asleep at night. Her body clock is regulated by internal factors like hunger and tiredness, as well as external ones, such as light and dark, and her day-to-day schedule.

● Her mental and social skills are developing so that she is able to recognize and respond to your cues. For example, if you give her a bath before bedtime every night, she will now have the capacity to remember that after a bath, it's time for her to settle down and go to sleep.

Expert tips

Between two and six months, your baby will give you cues that she is getting sleepy and is ready for a nap or bedtime. She may:

● decrease her level of activity and go quiet

● lose interest in people or toys

● start yawning

● rub her eyes

● look "glazed"

● become fussy or irritable

● bury her head in your chest or turn away from you.

Checklist

Your baby's bedtime routine can include any (or all) of the following activities:

- giving her a bath
- giving her a gentle massage
- putting on her sleepsuit
- reading a bedtime story
- singing to her
- cuddling her
- feeding her
- kissing her goodnight.

Helping your baby sleep

From around three months, you can help teach your baby to adopt healthy sleep patterns by doing two very important things:

- gently teaching her how to go to sleep by herself, and
- establishing a bedtime routine.

At some point, you will want your baby to feel secure enough to go to sleep and stay asleep without needing you there (see below). If she is able to do this, she will sleep better, which will have a positive impact on her physical and mental development. It also means that you and your whole family will reap the rewards – eventually – by having fewer disturbed nights.

Starting a routine

When your baby was a newborn, deciding when to put her down for the night was as easy as watching for the signs of sleepiness she gave, such as crying, yawning or rubbing her eyes.

While your baby may still do these things (and you should still respond to them), you don't need to wait for

Steps to a good night's sleep

1 For your baby to learn how to sleep by herself, she needs to be put to bed while she is still awake. Instead of rocking her to sleep or allowing her to doze off while feeding, keep her awake: sing or talk to her in a soft voice, stroke her head, or cuddle her.

2 When she is drowsy, put her into her cot on her back. At first, she may become more awake and fuss or cry. Soothe her gently, say goodnight in a soft voice and leave.

3 If she cries, resist going back for a few minutes. If she carries on, go in to her, stroke her, but don't pick her up.

4 When she is calm, leave the room again. If she continues to cry, wait a little longer than last time, then repeat the soothing visit. You may have to do this many times, but if you are consistent, within a few nights she will be going to sleep by herself. Some babies go to sleep with the help of a soothing sensation, such as sucking a thumb or dummy (see page 25). Others prefer the feel of a soft toy or blanket. Never put your baby to bed with a bottle, as this can cause tooth decay.

5 If your baby wakes during the night, and she is not due a feed or crying out of pain or discomfort, repeat these steps, waiting for a few minutes before soothing her and leaving the room again.

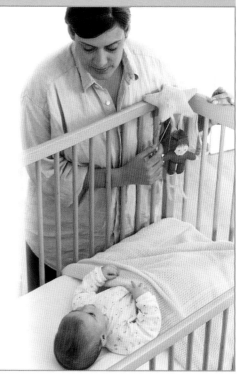

these signs before you put her to bed. You can now take more control of bedtimes, by putting her down at roughly the same time every night, with a similar routine.

To begin with, this will be a bit hit and miss because her feeding and napping habits can still be unpredictable. But introducing a routine now can go a long way towards regulating these patterns and setting her body clock to a healthy schedule.

She will probably respond well to routine at this stage, and enjoy the rituals of preparing for her night-time sleep.

The following tips will help you establish a bedtime routine that works for both you and your baby.

● **Choose your baby's bedtime –** and try to stick to it whenever possible. Normally, this will be any time between 7pm and 8.30pm. If you put her to bed any later than 8.30pm, there is a risk that she may become overtired.

● **Be consistent** Try to follow the same sequence of events at around the same time every evening.

● **Always keep your routine manageable** Elaborate routines can become drawn out indefinitely, which means that you will be spending longer than necessary settling your baby to sleep and defeats the object of the exercise.

● **Try to stick to a daytime routine, too** Your baby will now have longer periods of wakefulness

during the day, so you will have the opportunity to give the day more of a structure. Having regular times for playing, feeding and napping, for example, can be beneficial for you and your baby.

● **Be flexible** Having a routine doesn't mean you have to stick to it rigidly. It will vary sometimes, depending on what you're doing in the day and how tired your baby is. Be consistent, but know when to bend the rules.

How can I help my baby settle at night – and sleep through?

A bedtime routine helps your baby recognize that it's time to go to sleep – and the ideal time to start a simple routine is from around the age of three months. Once she is settled, there are steps you can take to ensure that she doesn't wake up unnecessarily.

Starting a routine

Think carefully about what you would like to include in your young baby's bedtime routine, because whatever you establish now may later become a habit that will be hard to break. You can always add to her routine as she gets older (see pages 42–43) but, for now, keep it simple. Your aim should be to create a peaceful, relaxing end to her increasingly busy day. Try the following:

★ **A warm bath** As well as a practical way of keeping her clean, a gentle splash in the water before bed can be enjoyable.

★ **A massage** Massage is known to boost a baby's feeling of wellbeing, and is a perfect way to help her relax before bed, especially after her bath.

★ **A cuddle and a feed** Once she's dressed, a cuddle and a good feed will help her go to bed contentedly. Try to ensure that you put her down awake, but drowsy.

A BATH
A bath can help your baby to wind down. Make sure the bathroom is warm and have a towel, a fresh nappy and her sleepsuit to hand. Wrap her up and give her a big hug!

Why is she waking?

Erratic sleep patterns are normal during the early months, but you can start to help your baby sleep through the night by considering why she's waking and trying to eliminate the cause.

★ **Is she hungry?** If she suddenly starts waking more frequently she may be having a growth spurt, which means she needs more milk to be sustained.

★ **Is she uncomfortable?** Always check that your baby is not in pain, that her nappy is not wet or soiled, or that she's not too hot or cold (see pages 20–21). Check for a temperature, and other signs of illness. If you suspect she is ill, call your doctor.

★ **Is she being disturbed?** If she sleeps in your room, she may hear you stirring, for example, so think about moving her to her own room.

★ **Is her room too dark or too light?** Your baby needs just enough light to reassure herself that she's in familiar surroundings. A simple night-light can solve this problem. Black-out curtains will help block out light.

★ **Are you sure she's really awake?** Sometimes, you may think your baby is waking when she's just in a phase of light sleep. Or she may be awake but about to drift back to sleep if not stimulated. When you know she's not ill or hungry, let her fuss for a few minutes before going to her.

★ **Can she fall asleep by herself?** Putting her down while drowsy but still awake will help her learn to fall asleep by herself (see page 32).

A MASSAGE
Massage your baby using light, circular or sweeping strokes all over her body, and a little baby oil if you wish. As you massage her, talk softly to her and maintain eye contact.

A CUDDLE AND A FEED
Make sure that the last feed your baby has before bedtime is a full feed, so that she doesn't wake up too soon feeling hungry. If she falls asleep before she has finished, try to rouse her.

Coping with early risers

If your baby regularly wakes up too early in the morning, you can sometimes solve the problem by putting black-out curtains or blinds on the window in her room to block out the morning light. Don't go to her straight away when she wakes up and fusses – leave her a while to see if she will go back to sleep.

Some paediatricians recommend helping your baby "readjust" her body clock, by keeping her up an extra hour at night, but there is no guarantee that this will work.

If you do try it, it's worth persisting for several nights to see if there is a difference to her waking time because any change won't take effect immediately.

Unfortunately, many babies and children are simply unable to sleep late in the morning and wake just because they have had enough sleep. You may have to adapt to her pattern for a while. At around six months, you can put some of her favourite toys in her cot to keep her occupied while you catch a few more precious minutes of sleep.

Daytime naps

The length and quality of your baby's daytime naps will affect her night-time sleep – and vice versa. By four or five months, the typical baby takes three or four regular naps of an hour or so each during the day. Some babies will take two longer ones of around 90 minutes or more.

Longer naps may be more beneficial for your baby; cat-napping during the day – falling asleep in sporadic bursts of half an hour or so – does not have the same effect, and your baby may follow the same pattern during the night, waking up frequently. So, try to encourage your baby to sleep better during the day.

● Aim to time her naps well. Having a nap too late in the day can mean that she won't sleep as well at night.

Questions & Answers

How do I know whether my baby is getting enough sleep?
Many babies regulate themselves pretty well when it comes to getting their quota of sleep, but not every baby gets as much as she needs. If she is frequently irritable and hard to please, it may be that your baby isn't napping enough or getting enough total sleep. If you believe your baby needs more sleep, try putting her down earlier, even if she cries for a while, and leaving her for a few minutes if she wakes in the night or too early in the morning to see if she goes back to sleep. But if she sleeps less than the "average" for her age and seems happy, then she's probably getting enough sleep and just happens not to need as much as other babies.

LONGER NAPS
It's better for your baby to have longer naps of good quality sleep, than to snatch several short sleeps during the day.

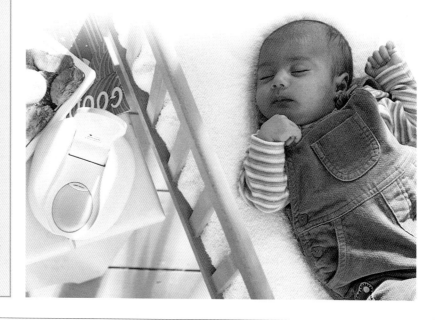

Incidentally, cutting down on daytime naps won't help her to sleep more at night – in fact, it can be a recipe for overtiredness and lead to your baby having a worse night's sleep.

● As soon as you know that your baby is tired, let her sleep. If she gets overtired, she may become irritable and find it very hard to sleep.

● Plan a nap routine to help her wind down. A feed or drink, a look at a book and a cuddle before putting her down will be enough.

● Make sure that she has a comfortable place to nap. Letting her fall asleep on your shoulder will be uncomfortable for you, and will mean that she doesn't sleep for long – her cot is better.

● Check that she isn't too warm or too cold (see pages 20–21).

● Try not to let her fall asleep just before her feed is due because she will probably wake up too soon out of hunger.

● Change her nappy before you put her down so that she feels comfortable as she settles.

● Play and interact with your baby when she's awake and active between naps. At five months, she should be able to stay awake for around three hours at a stretch – but with so much to hold her interest now, don't let her get overtired.

Snoring and noisy breathing

From around eight weeks, or sometimes before, some babies start to make "snoring" noises in their sleep. These are caused by loose mucus in the nose and throat (common in young babies) and may be accompanied by a rattling in her chest, which you may be able to feel with your hand. You may also notice a pause in your baby's breathing for a short period.

Some babies have more of a throat gurgle, usually the result of having a soft and flexible airway. This resolves itself within a year or two as the rings of cartilage in the airway become more rigid.

These snoring sounds do not usually interfere with your baby's breathing and will disappear over the next few weeks.

Always have any breathing irregularities, snores, gurgles or pauses in your baby's breathing checked by your doctor. Although it is unlikely to be a serious problem, other causes need to be ruled out. If your baby suddenly starts making strange breathing sounds or wheezes, see your doctor promptly.

"*I love it now that Megan's more active during the day, but she gets tired easily. So, as soon as she starts rubbing her eyes, I put her down.*"

SUE mum to six-month-old Megan

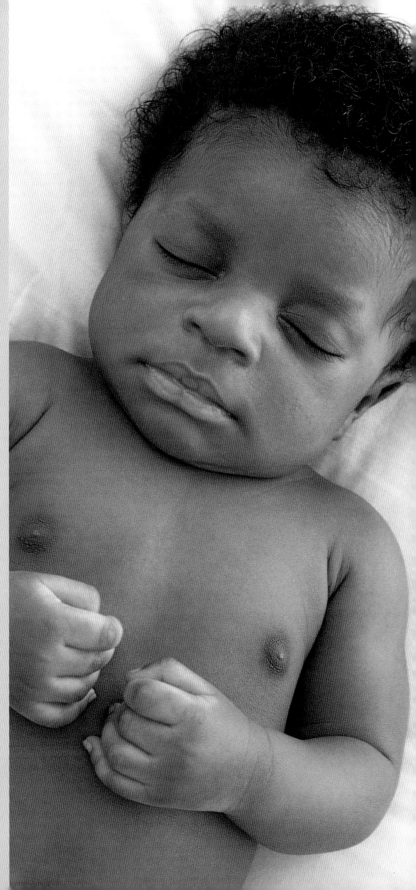

" Sonny's been so much **more settled** over the past few weeks – sometimes he'll go for five hours without waking. I love watching him as he sleeps. He looks like **an angel.** "

HANNAH is mum to six-month-old Sonny

The benefits of routine

By the time your baby is six months old, his world will be an endless source of fascination, and he will be wide awake and alert during play periods. While he's more likely to sleep well after these interludes of intense activity, he may be less willing to cooperate at naptimes or bedtime – after all, there are so many interesting things to do. This is when you will reap the rewards of having a daytime and bedtime routine.

Longer nights

From six months, your baby will be able to sleep for longer periods at night. He'll probably spend around 11 hours asleep at night, although this is unlikely to be all in one uninterrupted stretch.

At this stage, most babies also take two regular daytime naps of an hour or more (one in the morning and one in the afternoon) but patterns will vary considerably.

Although many babies settle nicely into a healthy sleeping routine at this stage, many more will go through periods of disrupted night sleep.

Separation anxiety

At some point during the second half of his first year, your baby may suddenly start to become tense and fearful around strangers; he may cry when you leave the room or give him to someone else to hold (even someone familiar to him), and he may seem more clingy than usual. This is known as separation anxiety, and it is an important step forward in your baby's emotional development.

Separation anxiety is a healthy indication that your baby is slowly becoming aware of his independence from you, which is both exciting and frightening for him.

Your baby may suddenly become difficult to settle. He may get upset when you leave him to go to sleep, and bedtime and night-time awakenings may suddenly become complicated by problems that up until now hadn't bothered him. He may also be uncharacteristically frightened by loud noises or changes to routine, and he may start to wake at night and cry for you.

Checklist

There are several new reasons for night waking in babies aged from around six months.

• Your baby reaches many important developmental milestones during this period, and this may temporarily disrupt his sleep, particularly when he is acquiring his gross motor skills.

• Some connection between sleeping and eating remains, but the link is not as strong as it was. He no longer needs to feed at night, for example, so night feeds should be curtailed with your help (see page 40).

• Any changes to your baby's routine, for example a new childcare arrangement, illness or moving house, may temporarily disrupt sleep.

• Your baby now has a growing sense of being an individual, and may wake up and miss you in the night.

• He's now able to stay awake at will.

This is a normal and temporary phase, so stick to your routines as much as possible. Be extra loving and attentive towards your baby during the day, and keep night-time interactions with him supportive and caring, but brief and matter of fact.

It may be tempting to take him into bed with you as he goes through this phase, but you could be storing up trouble if you expect him to sleep in his own bed afterwards. Although you may have to go into his room more frequently during this period to reassure him with calming words or a gentle stroke, at other times he may settle if you simply call out to let him know you are near. A comforting or "transitional" object (see page 44) may help him now.

SETTLING HER BACK TO SLEEP
Keep night-time interactions with your baby brief. Speak softly to her, perhaps stroke her hand, but don't pick her up.

Any changes to your baby's daily routine may lead to a period of increased waking during the night (see pages 56–61). One significant change that could happen around this time is your return to work. As well as missing you, your baby will be coping with a new childcare arrangement. If he goes to day nursery, he may have to adapt to a new nap routine and the extra stimulation of a busy environment.

You may want to keep your baby up for a while when you come home from work. You can prepare for this before you return to work by moving his bedtime back gradually. But, again, stick to his usual routine, and a bedtime of no later than 8.30pm.

Avoiding overtiredness

Until now, there wasn't much to keep your baby up at night. But with so many new discoveries to make, toys

Dropping night feeds

From around six months, your baby no longer needs to be fed during the night. He may drop his night feeds himself, but it's more likely that he will need your help. The best way of doing this is to progressively reduce the amount of milk he has during night feeds. Stopping suddenly is not advisable – although your baby wouldn't suffer nutritionally, he has learnt to wake up expecting to be fed. You need to re-train him so that he no longer associates waking up or falling asleep with feeding. The following is only a suggestion, but one that has worked for many parents.

● **If you are breastfeeding**, you can judge how much milk your baby is getting by the number of minutes he spends at the breast. Reduce this by a minute each night, and increase the periods between feeds by half an hour.

● **If bottle-feeding**, put 30ml (1fl oz) less in the bottle for night-time feeds. Decrease by the same amount every night, and increase the time between feeds by half an hour.

● **When your baby wakes up** and it's not time for a feed, comfort him, but don't hold him. Pat him or speak to him softly, then leave the room once he is calm.

● **Enlist the help of your partner.** If you are breastfeeding, your partner may have more success in settling your baby than you because your baby won't be agitated by the smell of your milk.

It may take several days, but if you persevere, your baby will learn that his night wakings will not be rewarded with a feed and should sleep through as a result.

to play with, and physical skills to perfect, your baby may not want to take time out to sleep.

Because his brain no longer simply "shuts down" when he's tired, he is able to stay awake even when he needs to sleep. Missing naps or going to bed late will make him irritable and may stop him from settling down, as well as make him more likely to wake during the night.

So, to prevent your baby becoming overtired, be consistent in your approach to his daytime naps and bedtime routines. Even if he doesn't seem tired, go through his usual calming bedtime rituals with him. Don't wait until he seems really tired before trying to settle him – putting him to bed calm and in a good mood is far more effective than if he's agitated and tearful.

CHECKING YOUR BABY
If you want to check that your baby's sleeping soundly during the night, always try to do so from the door of his room to avoid disturbing him if he's in a light stage of sleep.

" *Often, Callum cries for me to stay as he falls asleep. To break the habit, each night I move further from his cot until I'm outside, and out of sight!* "

EVE is mum to 13-month-old Callum

What is a good bedtime routine for my 10-month-old?

The benefits of having a well-established bedtime routine in place for your baby at this stage cannot be over-emphasized. If you're not sure what to include in your baby's bedtime routine, try some of the suggestions here. Experiment and see what works best for you and your baby.

Bedtime routines

A regular bedtime routine will:

★ give her the signals she needs that the day is over and that it's time to wind down and go to sleep

★ help to promote healthy and peaceful sleeping habits

★ give your baby a real sense of security

★ become an enjoyable and fulfilling part of your relationship for many years to come

★ help you to settle your baby after there's been some kind of disruption in her life, such as illness, a house move, or perhaps when staying away from home.

From now on, it's a good idea to feed your baby before you begin her bedtime routine. This will help

IT'S STORYTIME
Reading together is the perfect opportunity for a cuddle before bedtime, as well as encouraging in your baby a love of books.

her to disassociate sleeping with feeding and it means she won't fall asleep at the breast or bottle. Learning to go to sleep without you is an invaluable skill. You could try some or all of the following in your baby's bedtime routine.

★ **Give her a bath** A bath is not just a way to keep your baby clean – it is warming and relaxing.

★ **Clean her teeth** Remember to do this every night after her last feed.

★ **Dim the lights** When it's time to put on her pyjamas or sleepsuit, draw the curtains in her bedroom, dim the lights and keep noise levels low. Any distractions should be kept to a minimum.

★ **Tell her a story** Settle down together and spend some quiet time looking at a book. Read to her, look at the pictures and let her explore the book and turn the pages if she likes.

★ **Give her a cuddle** A goodnight kiss and cuddle before you lift her into her cot ready for sleep will be a pleasurable end to the day for you both. Place your baby's favourite soft toy or blanket in her bed to help comfort her.

★ **Say goodnight** Once your baby is settled, leave the room. If she stirs or cries, wait a few minutes to see if she settles again. If she doesn't, go in to settle her, say goodnight again and leave.

CLEAN HER TEETH
Cleaning her teeth before bed is a useful sign that sleep time is near – and it teaches her good habits about looking after her teeth.

HAVE A BATH
With plenty of bath toys to amuse her, a bath is a fun and relaxing way to wind down before bed.

Getting ready for bed

Once you have established your baby's bedtime routine, it's worth building in some time beforehand to allow him to wind down from the day's activities.

It's a good idea to avoid boisterous activities and watching television in the hour or so before bedtime. Choose something soothing instead, such as looking at a book together. Other ways to ensure that your baby is ready to settle at bedtime include:

• avoiding giving him a heavy meal or a lot to drink before bedtime; a light snack or small drink is plenty

• not letting him fall asleep over his last feed, so that you can put him to bed awake but sleepy

• never leaving your baby with a bottle in his bed, as this can cause ear infections and tooth decay

• once you've put him down, avoiding rushing in to him at the first sound you hear, unless he really is in distress – if you leave him a few minutes he may settle down on his own.

Comfort objects

Between the ages of eight and 15 months, your baby may become attached to a certain object, such as a cuddly blanket or soft toy. These comforters are known as "transitional objects", and can help smooth the emotional passage from dependence to independence,

Ella won't settle to sleep without her special blanket. She takes it with her to bed, and always looks for it during the day when she's tired or feeling unsure. I'm glad that she finds it such a comfort.

CLAIRE is mum to 13-month-old Ella

especially when your baby is going through the developmental phase known as separation anxiety (see page 39). Having a comforting, familiar transitional object to snuggle up with or cling on to:

• reassures your baby when he's away from you
• helps him feel at home whenever he's in a strange place
• calms him down whenever he's feeling upset
• helps him relax into sleep.

Many parents find these comfort objects very helpful and actively encourage such an attachment, so that the chosen object becomes an indispensable companion for their child. You may want to keep a duplicate so that you can wash and dry one while the other is in use, and to be sure that you always have a replacement if the precious original is ever lost.

You will find that your baby will gradually give up his comfort object on his own as he finds more mature ways to deal with life's challenges.

For some babies, a dummy is a transitional object, but it's advisable to wean your baby off a dummy before he comes to rely on it as a part of his comforting routine.

Dummies at this stage can interfere with the development of your baby's language skills, may lead to more disturbed nights, and can be a difficult habit to break in later years (see page 25).

Questions & Answers

My seven-month-old bangs his head against the cot as he settles to sleep. Is this normal?
From around six months or so, a small percentage of babies and young children develop a habit of banging their heads against their cot bars or mattress, or indulge in some other repetitious, rhythmic activity, such as rocking themselves to sleep. While it may look alarming, this behaviour is not usually a sign that anything is wrong. It may last weeks, months or even years, but should have stopped by the age of three. If your baby is happy and isn't bruising himself, don't worry. But if head banging takes up a lot of his time, if he displays other unusual behaviour or is developing slowly, see your doctor.

Coping with teething

Teething is often blamed for night waking, but in many cases this is a false diagnosis. Your baby's first teeth will appear between five and 10 months, and this coincides with the onset of waking for other developmental reasons.

Symptoms of teething include mild irritability and dribbling. The gums around the emerging teeth may be swollen and tender, and he may want to bite on something firm, such as a teething ring, his fist or your finger. Talk to your doctor if your baby is clearly uncomfortable.

It's important not to blame teething every time your baby seems more unsettled than usual in case he is ill. A slightly raised temperature is normal when teething, but a temperature of 38°C (100.4°F) or more will not be caused by teething, and nor will diarrhoea or vomiting. In these cases, see your doctor.

MAKING IT BETTER
Gently massaging your teething baby's gums with your fingertip can help to soothe his discomfort.

" Molly used to **nap in her buggy** on the way to meet her brother from school, so she wouldn't go to bed until late. We then started **walking** her to school, and now she settles to sleep at 7.30pm. "

MICK, dad to three-year-old Molly

6

Sleep and your toddler

Don't be too surprised if bed comes top of the list of places your toddler would least like to be. Bedtime involves relinquishing toys, family and fun – so your efforts to put her down for the night may be met with considerable protest. She's slowly learning to be independent and to express herself with words (or with tantrums!), and she now has very definite opinions of her own.

Now that she is in her second year, your toddler may be sleeping for considerable stretches at night. But she is going through many developmental changes, and these may affect her sleeping patterns in new ways. Changes to her routine, such as starting playschool or nursery, are also very likely to have an impact on her sleep, and you may find that bedtime becomes a very different experience.

Happy bedtimes

At this stage in your child's life, anxieties and insecurities are a natural part of growing up. One of the best things you can do to help your toddler feel secure and to sleep well is stick to her regular bedtime routine. Not only will this be a source of reassurance and stability in her changing world,

but it will also play a crucial role in helping her to unwind after all the excitement and activity of a typical toddler day.

If, despite sticking to her regular routine, you find that she resists going to bed and bedtime becomes a battleground, there are a few things worth considering that may help to smooth the way.

● **Is she going to bed too early?** Putting a toddler to bed if she's really not tired can be futile. If she takes an hour or so to fall asleep, try pushing her bedtime back half an hour or so to see if it helps.

● **Would a comforter help?** If she doesn't have one already, you could try offering your toddler a comfort object, such as a soft toy, at bedtime. This can ease the transition from being awake with you and being asleep without you.

Daytime naps

Between the ages of one and three, your toddler will probably go from having two naps during the day to none at all.

● At 12 months, most babies will still be having two daytime naps, usually spread fairly evenly through the day – one in the morning and one in the early afternoon.

● At around 18 months, she may go through a brief stage when two naps are too many but one nap is not enough (see page 49).

● By the end of her second year, most toddlers can – and do – get by with just an afternoon nap, usually after lunch.

● At around three years, she may again go through another temporary stage when one nap is too much but she's not yet ready to cope with no nap at all.

Dropping daytime naps

As your toddler naturally drops one of her daytime naps, she may seem cranky around the time that she used to nap. However, this should pass once her body clock adjusts to the new routine.

You could try moving her lunch forward a little so that she has her afternoon sleep a bit earlier. It's also a good idea to establish a quiet period around the time she used to nap, maybe reading a story to her or listening to music.

If your child sleeps well at night, appears well rested in the morning and is generally good-natured all day, she's probably getting enough sleep. But if she continues to be irritable and overtired, easily frustrated and clumsy at her usual naptime or in the evening, you may find you need to revert to two naps for a while.

- **Does she need you with her while she falls asleep?** Do beware of becoming your child's comfort object. Unless she's having problems such as nightmares (see page 54), resist staying with her while she falls asleep, because she'll learn to expect your presence every night. Take your time getting her comfortable, giving lots of hugs and kisses, perhaps tidy up her room a little while she's settling, and then bid her goodnight. Don't ignore her questions and requests, but respond quickly and briefly. Let her chatter for a minute or two, then say goodnight and leave the room.

- **Has she got everything she needs?** Try to anticipate special requests in advance, so that bedtime isn't stretched out unnecessarily. Have a small cup of water waiting by her bed and everything else set up the way she likes it (night-light on, the door ajar, for example). And make sure she's not hot or cold, wet or hungry before putting her down.

- **Are you expecting too much?** Don't insist on your toddler going to sleep immediately if she says that she's not tired. Let her have her

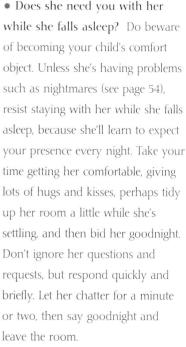

BEST FRIENDS
A treasured teddy bear, or other soft toy, to cuddle up to in bed could give your toddler the security she needs if she wakes in the night missing you.

A DRINK BEFORE BEDTIME
A drink from a beaker as part of his "wind-down" routine before bedtime is a good idea, but brush his teeth afterwards.

own quiet time, looking at books or listening to tapes in her room with the lights down. But do insist that she stays in bed.

● **Is her bedroom a nice place to be?** Never send your toddler to her room or her bed as a punishment. If you do, she may start to have difficulties seeing bedtime as pleasant. Also, let her have a say in how her room looks or where her special belongings are kept, so that she feels it's her own personal space.

Balancing day and night

Your toddler typically needs around 11 hours of sleep a night but, sometimes, bedtime battles and night-time problems can be caused by your toddler's daytime sleep schedule. For example:

● **Late-afternoon naps.** Having a nap too late in the afternoon may mean that she's unable to fall asleep again until late in the evening. Try not to let your child nap after around 4pm. If this means having to bring her naptime forward, try to do it gradually. Make her naptime 10 or 15 minutes earlier every day until it is at a more reasonable hour (say, 2pm). Your toddler will eventually adjust.

● **Not enough naps will leave your toddler overtired.** Decreasing or eliminating naps will not necessarily lead to easier bedtimes or better sleep. If your toddler becomes overtired, she's more likely to find it hard to sleep at night and may wake up more frequently.

● **Too many naps will also affect her night-time sleep.** By the age of two, many children have given up their morning naps, and will just have a sleep after lunch. If your toddler continues to nap twice a day, and you think this is affecting the way she sleeps at night, you may need to drop one.

Checklist

If your toddler is an early riser:

● she may not be getting enough sleep at night and is using her morning nap to catch up. This could be the case if she's irritable and wants to nap within two hours of waking. Gradually postpone her morning nap by 10 minutes each day until it becomes a mid-morning nap

● her bedtime may be too early. Re-adjust her bedtime by 10 minutes a day until you reach the ideal time. Don't expect immediate results – it will take your toddler's body clock a while to adapt

● daylight could be disturbing her. If you think this may be the case, invest in some thick curtains or black-out blinds to shut out the light

● she may be used to an early breakfast, so she'll learn to wake up for food at that time. Try to postpone her breakfast until a reasonable hour

● she may have a wet nappy. Avoid giving your toddler a lot to drink before bedtime

● she's had enough sleep, and is naturally an early riser. If this is the case, encourage her to play quietly in her room for a while, looking at books or playing with safe toys on her bed or in her cot.

Questions & Answers

My daughter is two and a half and keeps waking up at night and coming into our bedroom. What can I do?

When you put her to bed at night, explain to her that this is where she sleeps and that you will be in your own bed, too. Make sure you put her down while she is awake and leave her room before she has drifted off. If she calls you, or gets out of bed, quietly reassure her with minimum fuss or take her back to her room. Settle her quickly and leave again. Letting her stay in your bed, even if it's after the fifth time she's come in, will only teach her that this is acceptable. Some parents don't mind their children coming in to them during the night, but if you do, you need to be reassuring, firm and consistent in taking her back to her own bed. Your sleep may be disturbed for several nights, but your toddler will eventually get the message.

TIME FOR BED
It's a big step for your toddler to move up from his cot to a big bed. Take your cues from him and make the change when he's ready.

Ready for a "big bed"

At some point before or around the age of three, you'll want to move your toddler from her cot into a bed. There is no set age for doing this; you will probably know when she's ready. She may already be climbing out of her cot, expressing an interest in having a big bed, or she may need independent access to her potty at night, for example. Many toddlers are thrilled at the prospect of moving to a grown-up bed. But change of any kind can be daunting for your child, and there may still be a small part of her that wants to hang on to her last remaining link with babyhood. You can help your toddler make the transition from cot to big bed.

• **Be sure the time is right.** If your toddler is not yet ready, or is unsettled – for example, if she's just started nursery – postpone the move until things are more stable for her.

• **Tell her about her new bed** – don't spring it on her without warning. Talk about friends of hers who sleep in beds, look at pictures of children getting into bed.

• Let her help you choose her bed – and some special bedlinen to go on it.

• When you get the bed, leave her old cot in the room for a while, if there's space. This will help her to get used to it.

• Let her get to know her new bed for a few days first. You could let her play in it and have cuddles and read stories or nap in it, before urging her to sleep in it at night.

• If you need her cot for your new baby, make sure you get your toddler used to her big bed before moving the baby into the cot, so that your toddler doesn't feel she's being ousted by her sibling.

• Take your cues from your toddler. If she's excited by the idea of her bed, remove the cot from her room. But if she seems hesitant, give her the extra time she needs to make the transition.

Expert tips

There are a number of precautions to take to ensure that your toddler is safe in her new bed.

• Install guard rails on both sides of the bed, even if one side is up against the wall.

• Unless the guard rails run the length of the bed, cushion the floor with a rug, mattress or row of pillows in case she falls out.

• Clear away furniture and large toys that could injure her if she gets up.

• If necessary, install a safety gate across her bedroom door to keep her from wandering around the rest of the house while you are asleep.

• If you haven't done so already, put childproof latches on windows, cupboards and chests of drawers and secure furniture that could topple, such as a bookcase, to the wall.

" *I love reading to Rosie before bed – it's our special time. She always snuggles up and smells so sweet from her bath. It's a perfect end to the day.* "

FIONA is mum to 20-month-old Rosie

" Every night, I used to have to check for monsters in Eva's room before she would go to bed. Now she's **sharing a room** with her sister, and her fear of scary things has **disappeared.** "

JAMES, dad to four-year-old Eva

7

The pre-school years

Your child is probably constantly on the go during the day, so his nights may now be relatively peaceful, although there may be times when vivid dreams awaken him. This is because, during this period, he is becoming far more aware of himself and his relationships with other people as he tries to make sense of how the world works.

How much sleep?

Your child will need at least 10 to 12 hours of sleep each night, and he may still need to top this up with a daytime nap.

At this age, children are very good at keeping themselves awake, even when they are feeling exhausted. If your child is often irritable during the day, the chances are that he's tired because he's not getting enough sleep at night. Inadequate sleep is also often linked with aggressive or impulsive behaviour, "hyperactivity" and inattentiveness. It's therefore important to make sure that he is regularly getting enough sleep at night.

The best way of doing this is by sticking to his set bedtime. Even if your child appears to be full of energy in the evening, try to establish a quiet period before it's time for bed. Reading some books together, playing a quiet game or just having some cuddles on the sofa can help him wind down as part of his bedtime routine.

Getting ready for bed

Refusing to go to bed is one of the most common problems parents of pre-schoolers have to face. Your child may be too involved in what he's doing to want to go to bed. He may want to test the rules to see how much he can get away with, or there may be other reasons for avoiding sleep, such as imaginary monsters or fear of the dark (see page 54).

To avoid arguments, try warning your child a few minutes before it's time to go to bed. You could even set a kitchen timer to go off about 10 minutes before you plan on starting the bedtime routine, so he learns to associate this with finishing his game and mentally preparing himself for bed. Introduce clearing away his toys as part of his routine.

Expert tips

Now that your child has passed the toddler stage, he is mature enough to understand your reasoning. To make bedtimes easier, try the following.

● Explain to him that sleep is necessary to have the energy to play and run and have fun.

● Remind him that everyone goes to sleep at night – his friends, grandparents, or favourite fictional characters, for example.

● Make his bedroom a pleasant place to be. At this age, he will appreciate having somewhere that is his own special space. Help him decorate it with his favourite pictures, let him choose the colours of his bedclothes and walls, and get him involved in decisions about his room, such as where he'd like things kept. If he enjoys being in his room, he's far more likely to want to stay in it.

Checklist

Like night terrors, sleepwalking occurs when a child partially comes out of a deep sleep. Most children grow out of it by the age of six.

- There is no need to rouse your sleepwalking child – in fact, it may alarm him if you do. Instead, gently guide him back to bed.

- Make sure your home is safe (with window locks and safety gates) and there are no hazards, such as toys, that he could trip over. It may be useful to hang a bell on his door so you know if he leaves his room.

- Other common forms of harmless sleep behaviour include sleeptalking and grinding teeth.

Fertile imaginations

Children of this age have very fertile imaginations, which can run riot at bedtime. If your child thinks there are monsters or other scary things in his room, it's important to take his fears seriously – they are real to him – and to let him know he is safe.

Turn on the light to show him that his room at night is just as cosy as it is during the day. He may prefer to keep his light on for the rest of the night, or you could leave a light on outside his door or use a night-light, if you haven't done so already.

If he's afraid of what he thinks might be lurking behind cupboard doors or under his bed, do a thorough "monster check". You need to be sensitive to his concerns, but help him to see that there's nothing to be afraid of. This will help him feel confident and secure enough to go to sleep.

Waking at night

If your child is woken up by a nightmare (see box) or is in pain or distress, go to him straight away and reassure him. But at other times, you need to deal with his night wakings with the minimum of fuss.

If your child calls out to you in the night, you could try reassuring him by calling back to him that you are there, "It's alright, Mummy's here. Go back to sleep." The next time he calls, leave it a bit longer before answering

Having a nightmare

All children have nightmares and they are particularly common among pre-schoolers. These scary dreams may relate to something that has happened during the day, or to fears that come to the surface by way of images or dreams.

If your child has had a nightmare, he will wake up, afraid and crying. Comfort him as quickly as possible – he'll need lots of reassurance from you. If you can, get him to talk about the dream, and try making up a happier ending. Stay with him until he's calm.

Although distressing for you, nightmares are rarely serious. By the time he's five or so, he'll be better able to understand that these images are only dreams, but younger children will still need to be reassured that they are not real.

him to give him the chance to fall back to sleep on his own. This is not the time to lavish him with attention, as it will only keep him awake and he will come to expect it next time. If you do need to go to his room to put him back to bed, be brisk with your goodnights.

Your child may awaken crying for reasons other than nightmares. Check for fever and any symptoms that may suggest an ear infection, stomach upset or another illness. Call your doctor if you are concerned.

" Harry has always been an early riser. I think it's because his daddy has to get up early for work during the week and he hears him moving about. "

AMANDA is mum to three-year-old Harry

WAKING EARLY
If your toddler comes in to your room before it's time to get up, try to persuade her to go back to bed and play quietly.

Dealing with night terrors

Night terrors are far less common than nightmares, but they tend to happen most frequently during the pre-school years. If your child is having a night terror, he will seem to be wide awake (even though he's not) and upset, perhaps crying, screaming or thrashing, but not responding to you. He'll have no recollection of it the next day.

Try holding your child and reassuring him, but don't attempt to wake him as this may aggravate him more. After a while, he'll settle and go back to sleep. Night terrors are not damaging and they soon pass. They are often more scary for parents to witness than for a child to experience. Your child will stop having them as he gets older.

" Jamie suddenly started to **wake up** in distress every night, and the doctor diagnosed an ear infection. He had antibiotics to clear it up, and has **slept peacefully** ever since. **"**

SARAH is mum to two-year-old Jamie

Special situations

Once your child has learned how to fall asleep by herself, she will probably continue to sleep well. But occasional disruptions to her sleep patterns are inevitable. Illnesses, going on holiday or other temporary changes in her life mean that there will be times when increased flexibility with her routine is essential.

The effect of illness

When your baby or child is ill, her nights may be punctuated by frequent wakings. Discomfort from vaccinations, fever, pain, coughing, or a stuffy nose are all possible contenders for keeping her awake at night.

Your baby will need soothing, cuddling, drinks, medication (if appropriate) and lots of comfort. You may find it easier to sleep in with her while she is ill, as she may want extra feeds or cuddles during the night, and it can be reassuring to know that you are close at hand.

Giving your child the attention and comfort she needs is most important at this stage. But as soon as she is well again, you need to pick up your usual night-time routine in order to avoid any long-term sleep problems.

● **Colds and snuffles** If your baby develops a cold, it may upset her sleep. A blocked nose will force her

to breathe through her mouth, and this can interfere with self-soothing techniques, such as thumb-sucking.

Also, feeding can be difficult with a blocked nose and your baby may give up before she's fully satisfied, meaning that she will be hungry again soon afterwards and in need of another feed. Many babies seem to prefer to feed little and often when they are ill.

The best thing you can do for your baby or child is to help her feel as comfortable as possible. Wipe her nose gently when necessary. A little smear of petroleum jelly under her nose may ease any soreness. Make sure that her room is the ideal temperature of 18°C (65°F). A cool-mist humidifier in her room may help to keep her nasal passages clear, or try a few drops of an over-the-counter menthol inhalant on a handkerchief in her bed.

When she's ill

Always call a doctor:

● if your baby is under three months and has a temperature of 38°C (100.4°F) or more

● if your baby or child has severe or persistent symptoms at any age.

Remember, if your baby or child wakes up crying at night, the very first thing you need to do is make sure she is not ill – never leave her to cry or try to start any kind of sleep training programme if she is unwell.

FEELING ILL
She needs you most of all when she's ill, so be sure to respond quickly when she wakes at night.

• **Ear infections** Ear infections can have a profound effect on your child's sleeping habits. These common complaints often go undiagnosed but are a major cause of disturbed nights in babies and young children.

An ear infection is painful, and it may wake your baby or child frequently. In some cases, the pain is believed to be caused by the build-up of fluid in the middle ear, which cannot drain away adequately when your baby is lying down.

If she has an ear infection your child may be grizzly, possibly go off her feeds, pull her ears, and you may notice a discharge. She will seem unsettled and difficult to comfort.

If you suspect that your baby or child has an ear infection, take her to see your doctor without delay.

Getting back to normal

Temporary changes to bedtime routines and night-time arrangements on a trip or during illness are unavoidable and necessary, and if you re-establish your routine as soon as possible after the disruptive period, you should avoid long-term problems. If your child remains unsettled after everything else has returned to normal, then you may need to go back to the sleep training technique described on page 32.

Never be tempted to offer your baby or child any over-the-counter medication that causes drowsiness in an attempt to "cure" her sleep problems. If her sleeplessness is severe, see your doctor or health visitor, who will give you advice or may suggest that you visit a sleep clinic (see page 61).

In the meantime, infant paracetamol syrup (for babies over three months) can ease pain and reduce any accompanying fever. Follow your doctor's instructions for dosage.

Prescribed medication may be necessary: ear infections respond very well to treatment. Once your child's ear infection has been treated, she will sleep better, and so will you.

Going on holiday

Going on holiday, or staying in other people's homes, often means having to compromise your daytime and sleep routines. For example, your baby may have to share your room, or sleep in an unfamiliar cot or bed. You may need to respond to her differently when you are away from home – for instance, you might need to go to her quickly if she wakes in the night so that she doesn't wake

A DAY BED
When she's ill, you may want to keep her near you during the day, so make her bed up on the sofa.

everyone else up, whereas at home you might leave her for a few minutes to see if she goes back to sleep by herself.

Temporary changes like these are fine, as long as your child gets back to her usual schedule for play, meals and sleep when she returns home. Any disturbance in her sleep/wake cycle will probably disappear in a few days.

The key to having the whole family sleep well on holiday or when visiting friends or relatives is to temper the novelty of a new environment with some of the familiar sensations that your child finds comforting (see above right).

Expert tips

There are several steps you can take to minimize upset to your baby or child's routine when sleeping away from home.

● Remember to take her comfort object with you, if she has one.

● Take her blanket or pillow from home so that she has something familiar in bed with her.

● Try to keep to her normal sleep/wake routine as much as possible.

● If the holiday involves travel to a different time zone, adopt local time from the moment you arrive, but be prepared to allow for naps at odd times to make up for sudden fatigue.

● As soon as you are home, revert to your regular routine and bedtime.

TRAVEL COT
A travel cot is invaluable if you often stay away. Follow the usual safety advice (see pages 20–21).

Questions & Answers

How can I help my two-year-old son acclimatize when the clocks go forward or back?

Putting your clock forward, or back, may disrupt your child's sleeping patterns for a few days. But the best way to help him adapt is to go with the "new" time from the outset. When the clocks move forward in the spring, bedtime will be an hour earlier, and he may be wide awake at bedtime and take longer to go to sleep for a while. When the clocks go back in winter, he may be falling asleep by bedtime. You could try moving your child's bedtime 15 minutes earlier – or later in the spring – every evening to help him cope with the change gradually. Accept that these temporary hiccups will occur and your child will soon adapt his sleeping patterns.

Wetting the bed

Most children are toilet trained by the age of three, and dryness usually follows soon afterwards. But as many as 15 per cent of pre-schoolers still frequently wet the bed up to the age of five, or even later.

If your child still wets the bed after toilet training has been well established, it may be simply that she is a bit later than average in developing the ability to wake up when she senses her bladder is full. The problem is very likely to clear up as she matures.

If your child suddenly starts to wet the bed at night after having been dry for some time, the cause could either be a urinary tract infection, for which she may need treatment, or she may be feeling some form of emotional stress. Starting school for the first time, the arrival of a new baby, or upset in the family, for example, may all result in this temporary problem.

If your child starts to wet the bed:

• reassure her, be sympathetic and provide the emotional support she needs; look for the cause of the stress and try to reduce her exposure to it

• don't make a fuss or tell her off or punish her – it's not her fault

• use a waterproof sheet, and keep plenty of clean bedlinen and nightwear handy

• when accidents do occur, let her help with changing sheets, but don't make it a punishment

STAYING DRY
Help your child feel comfortable and confident by putting a waterproof sheet on his bed and keeping his potty within easy reach.

● if she feels more secure wearing disposable pull-ups in bed for the time being, let her do so

● let other family members know that teasing will not be tolerated.

If the bedwetting continues for more than two weeks, or you cannot identify the source of the problem, see your doctor or paediatrician. If your child continues to wet the bed after the age of six, ask your doctor or paediatrician for advice.

Twins or more

With twins, or multiples, as with single babies, you'll find it a lot easier to get to grips with sleep problems once you've established a routine.

In the early days, try to get your babies on to the same schedule for feeding, playing and sleeping. Being organized is the key. Enlist as much help as you can – from your partner, family or friends, or even paid help if you can afford it.

Sleep problems among twins are frequently exacerbated because parents naturally rush into the bedroom at the first hint of noise, to stop one baby waking the other. While it is very tempting to react like this, it can store up problems for later. By responding so quickly, you may be unwittingly "teaching" your babies to wake up for a cuddle, feed or other form of attention.

Try to take a more relaxed approach to night-time waking. Surprisingly, many twins and multiples don't wake each other even when they cry at night. So, once the night-feeding phase is over, night-time wakings are best handled in the same way as recommended for single children (see page 32).

Where should twins sleep?

There are no particular rules about whether twins should sleep together or not. An arrangement that works for some won't work for others.

But most parents prefer to keep their twin babies together, at least to begin with. This usually works well and, as your babies become used to each other's company, they will learn to tune each other out and will remain asleep even if one or other twin wakes up crying.

If you wish to encourage a sense of individuality in your babies from the start, you may want to have them in separate rooms, space permitting. But you may find that your twins cry for each other and refuse to be parted at night. If this is the case, it's far better to follow their lead and have them sleep contentedly with two cribs or cots in one room than to put them in separate rooms before they are ready.

For safety reasons, it is generally recommended that every baby should have an individual cot, crib or bed. Perhaps the best compromise is to have your babies sleeping in the same room in cots that are placed side by side, so that they can see each other. You may find that they thrive on each other's company on waking and going to sleep, and are a source of great comfort to each other.

Sleep clinics

An increasing number of parents are turning to sleep clinics for help and advice on dealing with severe sleep problems. These clinics can be found across the UK, and are run by either the NHS or by private consultants.

Sleep clinics help break poor sleep cycles by "re-training" both parents and children. After an initial consultation, you will normally be asked to make a detailed diary of your child's sleeping habits. This will then be studied, and new routines to help train your baby or child to sleep will be offered, along with advice, support and monitoring. To find a sleep clinic in your area, contact your health visitor or doctor.

Useful contacts

**Association for
Post-Natal Illness**
145 Dawes Road, London SW6 7EB
Tel: 020 7386 0868
www.apni.org
Advises, supports and provides
information on postnatal depression.

**Association of Breastfeeding
Mothers (ABM)**
Helpline (24 hours): 020 7813 1481
http://home.clara.net/abm
Gives mother-to-mother
breastfeeding support and
up-to-date breastfeeding information.

BLISS
68 South Lambeth Road,
London SW8 1RL
Helpline: 0500 618140
www.bliss.org.uk
Offers help and support to families
of premature and sick babies, funds
research and campaigns for the
improvement of neonatal service.

CRY-SIS
BM CRY-SIS, London WC1N 3XX
Helpline: 020 7404 5011
www.cry-sis.org.uk
Provides emotional support and
practical advice for parents
dealing with a baby's crying
and sleep problems.

**Foundation for the Study of
Infant Deaths (FSID)**
Artillery House, 11-19 Artillery Row,
London SW1P 1RT
Helpline: 0870 787 0554
www.sids.org.uk/FSID/
Offers support and education to

parents and professionals on
reducing the risk of Sudden Infant
Death Syndrome (SIDS).

Gingerbread
7 Sovereign Close, Sovereign Court,
London E1W 3HW
Helpline: 0800 018 4318
Office: 020 7488 9300
www.gingerbread.org.uk
Provides support and practical
help for lone-parent families.

Home-Start
2 Salisbury Road, Leicester LE1 5QR
Helpline: 0800 068 6368
Office: 0116 233 9955
www.home-start.org.uk
Provides training, information and
support to existing and potential
Home-Start schemes, which offer
support, friendship and practical help
to families with children under five.

La Leche League (GB)
PO Box 29, West Bridgford,
Nottingham NG2 7NP
Helpline (24 hours): 0845 120 2918
www.laleche.org.uk
Offers help and information to
mothers wishing to breastfeed.

**MAMA
(Meet-A-Mum Association)**
376 Bideford Green, Linslade,
Leighton Buzzard LU7 2TY
Tel: 01525 217064
www.mama.org.uk
Aims to help mothers who feel
depressed and isolated when their
babies are born, through local groups
of mothers sharing their experiences.

National Childbirth Trust (NCT)
Alexandra House, Oldham Terrace,
London W3 6NH
Tel: 0870 444 8707
NCT breastfeeding helpline:
0870 444 8708
www.nctpregnancyandbabycare.com
Provides support for pregnancy,
birth and early parenthood, and
gives information to enable parents
to make informed choices.

**NSPCC (National Society
for the Prevention of
Cruelty to Children)**
42 Curtain Road, London EC2A 3NH
Free confidential helpline:
0808 800 5000
Textphone: 0800 056 0566
www.nspcc.org.uk
UK's leading charity specializing
in child protection and the
prevention of cruelty to children.

Parentline Plus
Unit 520, Highgate Studios,
53-79 Highgate Road, London
NW5 1TL
Helpline: 0808 800 2222
www.parentlineplus.org.uk
Offers support and information to
anyone parenting a child.

**TAMBA (Twins and Multiple
Births Association)**
2 The Willows, Gardner Road,
Guildford GU1 4PG
Twinline: 0800 138 0509
www.tamba.org.uk
Encourages and offers support
to families and carers of twins,
triplets or more.

Index

A

active sleep 7
   see also REM sleep
amount of sleep needed 8-9,
   10, 23, 36
anxieties & fears 39-40, 47,
   54-5

B

back, sleeping on 19, 20
bedrooms 13, 49, 53, 61
beds & bedding 13-21, 59, 61
   cot-to-bed transition 19,
   50-1
bedside cots 15, 16
bedtime routines 11, 58
   2-6 months 31, 32-5
   7-15 months 42-3, 44
   toddlers & pre-school
   children 47-9, 53
bedwetting 60-1
benefits of sleep 8, 9
body clocks 9, 11, 31, 33, 36
breast- & bottle-feeding
   see feeds
breathing & breathing
   monitors 18-19, 37

C

car seats 19
clocks going forwards
   or back 60
co-sleeping 15, 16-17
colds & snuffles 57
colic 25
comfort objects *see*
   transitional objects
cots 14-15, 17, 59, 61
   cot-beds 15
   cot-to-bed transition 19,
   50-1
cradles 14, 15, 20, 27
crying 24-5
cycles of sleep 8

D

day beds 59
daytime naps *see* naps
deep sleep 8
disturbed nights 17, 29
dream sleep *see* REM sleep
dreaming 10, 54
drowsiness 8
dummies 25, 45

E

ear infections 58-9
early risers 36, 49, 55

F

fears & anxieties 39-40, 47,
   54-5
feeds 23-4, 27, 33, 57
   night feeds 13, 17, 29, 31, 40
feet-to-foot sleeping 20

H

head banging 45
holidays 59
hours of sleep needed 8-9,
   10, 23, 36

I

illness 11, 18, 45, 55, 57-9
inconsolable crying 25

L

light sleep 8, 35
looking after yourself 29

M

mattresses 14, 16, 21
medical advice 18, 21, 37, 57
medications 58, 59
"monster" checks 54
Moro reflex 24
Moses baskets 13-14, 17,
   20, 27
multiples & twins 61

N

naps 11, 19, 29, 59
   2-6 months 9, 36-7
   7-12 months 9, 39, 41
   toddlers 9, 47, 48, 49
need for sleep 8, 9
newborns 7, 8, 13-21, 23-9
night/day distinction 11, 28
night feeds 13, 17, 29, 31, 40
night waking 8, 35, 39, 45,
   50, 54-5
nightmares & night terrors
   54-5
non-REM sleep 7-8

O

over-heating 20, 21
overtiredness 11, 33, 37, 40-1,
   49, 53

P

patterns *see* sleep patterns
premature babies 10
pre-school children 53-5, 60-1

Q

quiet sleep 7
   see also non-REM sleep

R

rapid-eye-movement sleep *see*
   REM sleep
refusing to go to bed 47-9, 53
REM sleep 7, 8, 10, 18, 24
rocking cradles 14, 15
routines *see* bedtime routines

S

safety 14, 16, 17, 19, 20-1,
   51, 54
self-soothing techniques 8,
   11, 28-9
semi-awakenings 8
separation anxiety 39-40

sharing your bed 15, 16-17
SIDS *see* Sudden Infant Death
   Syndrome
sleep clinics 61
sleep cues 28, 31, 32
sleep cycles 8
sleep patterns
   2-6 months 9, 10-11, 31-7
   7-12 months 9, 10-11, 39-45
   disrupted 57-60
   newborns 7, 8, 9, 23-9
   premature babies 10
   toddlers 9
sleep-stage progression 8
sleep training 25, 32
sleeping arrangements 13-21,
   61
sleeping away from home 59
sleeping positions 19, 20
sleepwalking 54
smoking 16, 20
snoring 37
soothing newborns 25, 26-7
stages of sleep 7-8
startle reflex *see* Moro
   reflex
Sudden Infant Death
   Syndrome (SIDS) 19, 20-1
swaddling 28

T

teething 45
temperature 20, 21, 57
time changes 59, 60
toddlers 9, 19, 47-51
transitional objects 44-5,
   47, 59
travel cots 59
twins & multiples 61

W

waking periods, newborns
   23
wetting the bed 60-1

Acknowledgments

DK Publishing would like to thank Sally Smallwood and Ruth Jenkinson for the photography, Sue Bosanko for compiling the index and Alyson Lacewing for the proofreading.

Models
Natalie Heymer Legg, Simon with Oban Murrell, Bonita Chong, George with Harry Demosthenous, Lupia with Sophira Elliott, Thimmie with Emily Pickering, Kim Seltzer with Jackson Appelt, Kofinan Agyemang, Sarah with Rudi Berman, Kim with Carla Rabin, Joanna Rosenfeld and Katarina Henderson, Michael with Nia Thomas, Emma Hewson, Karen Jones with India O'Hagan Jones, Rebecca Da Silva, Eya Choudhury, Elena Marrai, Jenny Lau with Sabina Tsang, Eleftheria with Theo Angeli, Andy with Joe Worpole, Paul with Daisy Copperwaite, Ria Shah, Kay with Ben Whiteley, Lulu Manitaras with Paul Efstartiou, Maria with Jasmine Leitch, Angel Kennett-Smith, Sally with Harvey Barron, Xiaoyan with Jiawei Guan

Hair and make-up Louise Heywood, Victoria Barnes, Susie Kennett, Amanda Clarke

Picture researcher Anna Bedewell

Picture librarian Romaine Werblow

Picture credits
The publisher would like to thank the following for their kind permission to reproduce their photographs:
9: Bubbles: Jennie Woodcock.

All other images © Dorling Kindersley.
For further information see: www.dkimages.com.